How to Read
a History Book

The Hidden History of History

How to Read a History Book

The Hidden History of History

Marshall T. Poe

zero
books

Winchester, UK
Washington, USA

First published by Zero Books, 2018
Zero Books is an imprint of John Hunt Publishing Ltd., Laurel House, Station Approach,
Alresford, Hants, SO24 9JH, UK
office1@jhpbooks.net
www.johnhuntpublishing.com
www.zero-books.net

For distributor details and how to order please visit the 'Ordering' section on our website.

ISBN: 978 1 78099 729 2
978 1 78535 646 9 (ebook)
Library of Congress Control Number: 2016962870

A CIP catalogue record for this book is available from the British Library.

Design: Stuart Davies

Printed and bound by CPI Group (UK) Ltd, Croydon, CR0 4YY, UK

We operate a distinctive and ethical publishing philosophy in all
areas of our business, from our global network of authors to
production and worldwide distribution.

CONTENTS

This book is dedicated to Professor Don Smith of Grinnell College, who taught me by example that a little humor goes a long way in most serious discussions.

Preface

This is not a book about history. Rather, it's a book about history books. You might well ask, "Why would I want to read a book about history books?" That's a fair question. If you don't read history books, there's no reason at all. You can put this book down right now and save yourself some time and money. I'll get over it. But if you do read history books, then let me explain why you should read it.

I've been reading, writing, and talking with people about history for a quarter of a century. By and large, the people I've encountered have a pretty good grasp of what history is and what a history book is. The former is the past and the latter is a true story about the past. These two plainspoken, intuitive, commonsensical definitions of "history" drive over-thinkers absolutely nuts. History, they often object, can't be that simple. To prove that it's not, over-thinkers write long books called things like *Microhistory*, *Macrohistory*, *Metahistory*, *Hyperhistory*, *Quantumhistory* and so on. Now these books, though hard to read, are interesting if you are excited by parsing, arranging, and rearranging words. I confess I am enthused by these things, but that's because most of my friends are over-thinkers and that's the way over-thinkers roll. But I can tell you with considerable assurance that these books, individually or as a bunch, do no damage whatsoever to the plainspoken, intuitive, commonsensical idea that history is the past and a history is a true story about the past. You needn't take my word for it; you can just wade into these books and find out for yourself. Honestly, and with no disrespect to my colleagues, I would not recommend this option unless you happen to be unemployed or a graduate student. Instead, you could just think for a moment about every history book you have ever read. What was it about? The past. What form did it take? A story. There you have it: as good an inductive proof as one could ever want.

So people already know what history is whether they know they know or not (or, I should add, whether they have been convinced by over-thinkers that they *don't* know). That's not the problem. The problem is that most folks who read history books don't really have a firm grasp of what a history book is. I can hear you saying: "Of course I know what a history book is, you pretentious dolt. It's a book about history." True enough. That's a good definition of a history book. But if that's all you knew about what a history book is, then—and here's the punch line—you would not fully comprehend the true story contained in a history book. Everyone knows you should not judge a book by its cover. Fewer people realize that you should not judge a book by its contents, where "contents" means a set of words united into sentences placed one after another on a physical or electronic page. The Reverend Martin Luther King said, famously, that we should judge people not by the color of their skin but rather by the content of their character. The first part works for books; the last part doesn't. The measure of a book is not just what it says, but how it says it.

It's this part—the how—that is the problem. Most history readers never consider the how when they sit down to read about, say, Reverend Martin Luther King. It's hard to blame them for this neglect. After all, the interesting part of a history book is first and foremost the story it tells, not the ink and paper, bindings and pages, sentences and paragraphs, chapters and sections, footnotes and bibliographies. These things are media, not messages, and most history readers are rightly interested in messages. Yet we all know—or should know by now—that media themselves have messages built into them (and I don't mean when you play them backwards). These messages are often hidden, and almost always subtle, but they are there nonetheless. A simple example from the history of books demonstrates this verity. The Gospels were popular books in medieval Europe, as they are today in modern Europe. In terms of contents, the Gospels are the Gospels—Matthew, Mark, Luke, and John (allowing, of course, for some textual variation). But in terms of media, the medieval and modern versions are very different; each has its own story to tell. The medieval version was likely handwritten in Latin on something like velum by clergymen for other clergymen. The modern version was probably printed in some vernacular language like Russian on paper for purchase by consumers. The way a book is produced, the form it takes, and the way it is distributed all tell us something about what's "inside" and the society that produces it.

It follows that if you want to have a complete understanding of the content carried in a medium, you also have to understand something about the medium itself. To grasp what's "inside" a history book, you have to understand how history books are written, what form they take, and the way they are distributed among other things. In sum, to comprehend history—the past and stories about the past—you must comprehend the artifact "history book." And that is why you may want to read a book about history books.

The purpose of this book, then, is to give the reader some understanding of what a history book is in a kind of anthropological sense. We want to know about how our tribe (so to speak) began writing history books and when; about which tribe members write history books now and how; about the kinds of history books the tribe's history-writers write and for whom; about what form the tribe's history books take; about the tribe's history publishers, what they publish, and for whom; and, finally, about how the tribe uses the history books after they are published. Doubtless other questions will arise as we proceed, but this is a good start.

As I said at the onset, this book is not a history. I have no intention of telling you a true story about the past; rather, I want to tell you the whole truth about history books. If I "stuck to the facts" as a historian might, I could not accomplish that goal, at least in a very entertaining way. If, however, I allow myself a certain poetic license, I think I can get the job done and keep you, gentle reader, from turning on the TV. I have, therefore, opted to tell the whole truth about history books *via* a historical fiction. The setting of this fiction is, well, historical: our world, past and present, and more particularly the contemporary United States. Though I made nothing up about this setting, I will confess altering some names to avoid offence and nitpicking about what "actually happened." I've not changed the names very much, so I imagine most clever readers will easily guess who or what I'm actually talking about. The fiction I have put in this setting—that of Elizabeth Ranke—is, well, fictional: there is no Elizabeth Ranke, never was and never will be. She is not, however, exactly "fictional." Rather, she is a composite based on my observation of people in the historical profession. Who she is and what she does, as they say in the movies, are "based on actual events." She is typical, though she is not actual.

Enough throat-clearing. Now, without out further delay, let's meet our protagonist. She wants to write a history book.

Chapter 1

The History of History Books

We historians used to make up meaningful stories. Now we just write true ones.
—Reinhardt Friedrich Freiherr von Teufel

Elizabeth Ranke, nearly BA, is 21 years old. She's white, bright and, though awfully ambitious, polite. Her family lives in a smart suburb of a large city on the East Coast of the United States. Her father is a professor in the humanities at a mid-level college and her mother is a lawyer in a small downtown firm. She has one younger brother, Martin, and no further additions to the clan are planned. The family self-identifies as "middle class," but the Rankes rest comfortably in the top 10% of Americans in terms of wealth and the top 2% in terms of educational attainment. They always vote Democratic and know few people who don't. Elizabeth attended a top-ranked public high school, where she was an excellent student. Upon graduation, she matriculated at a "very selective" school, Twiddletwaddle College, in another city on the East Coast. She's a history major and will take her degree—with highest honors—next May. She works hard and has high expectations. Now, in her penultimate semester, she's thinking about graduate school. She wants to write a history book.

As we'll see, she will. But before we follow her from BA to PhD to published historian, we should pause to note that both Elizabeth's aspirations and the artifact she wants to produce are, historically speaking, rather novel. To us, historians and history books are just part of the early twenty-first-century American scenery. Like interstate highways, McDonald's, and MTV, the two have just "always" been there. That's probably what Elizabeth thinks at this stage in her career. Her parents know about historians and history books; her grandparents knew about historians and history books; and her great-grandparents, well, she doesn't really know much about them, but it seems reasonable to suppose they did as well. But the fact of the matter is that hers is not a very reasonable supposition at all. At the turn of the nineteenth century, the time when her great-grandparents would have been coming of age, historians and history books were rather unusual. For it was only then that the institutional machinery that produces historians and history books was being established in the United States. Had Elizabeth been in her great-grandmother's shoes, she almost certainly wouldn't have wanted to become a historian or to write a history book. Almost no one did or could.

This is not to say, of course, that prior to 1900 there were no historians or history books. Though it would be too much to claim that Herodotus is a household name (would that it were so), many college graduates will be able to say that he was a Greek historian who lived a very long time ago, probably in Greece. Some few of them may even be able to propose that he wrote a history book called, appropriately enough, *The Histories*. Though this dim recollection is only half-right, it's not all wrong. And importantly for our purposes it's right enough for us to be sure that people we would call "historians" were writing true stories about the past we would call "histories" long before we were born.

The act of writing history, and therefore "the historian" and "the history" in their generic senses, are not new. But the profession "historian" and what we're calling a "history book" are new. They were the product of a very specific time, place, and set of circumstances. This is important to bear firmly in mind, because the first step in comprehending the artifact called "history book" is the understanding that history books are not everywhere, always, and of necessity, but rather here, now, and contingent. This is what Elizabeth, still a novice in the trade, doesn't see and neither do most people who read history books. The truth, however, is that historians and history books are not to be found in most of the human past; until very recently, historians and history books were not to be found in most places on the globe, and it is entirely possible to conceive of a here-and-now present in which neither professional historians nor history books find any place. If Elizabeth were reborn at random in time and space, chances are overwhelming that she wouldn't want to be a historian or write history books. She probably wouldn't even know what these things were. Moreover, it is not hard to imagine an alternative—and not entirely impossible—reality located exactly when and where she was born though without historians or history books.

That, fortunately for me and my colleagues, is not what happened. Though it's very difficult to pinpoint the exact historical origins of anything (human events, alas, don't really work like that), it's not too much to say that Germans invented the modern historian and history book in the mid-nineteenth century. More accurately, they invented the modern research university. The word "research" is the important one here. Universities had existed in Europe for about 800 years when the Germans broke ground. But they were first and foremost religious institutions designed to teach novices (and not very many of them) about, well, religion. Naturally they taught other things—mostly, it seems, Aristotle—but Christianity infused them all. Since the truth of Christianity (and, for that matter, of Aristotle) was manifest, there was no real need to go digging around for *new* knowledge, and in most places such endeavors were actively discouraged. Some brave folks did research, and we know their names well, perhaps too well: Kepler, Copernicus, Galileo, Newton, and so on. They were exceptions. The rule was learning old stuff by rote. What else was required when everything worth learning had already been revealed in the Holy

Scripture or received from Aristotle?

By the early nineteenth century, however, a number of important, powerful people in Europe began to believe that finding out new things might just be a good thing. They'd seen some new things in action—calculus, steam engines, morphine—and thought that having more of them around would be (as we would say) "in the national interest." The Germans were the first among them. They took the university "brand" and, under it, built a machine designed to make researchers and research instead of copiers and copies. The cogs and widgets of this machine included several key items, all of which are ubiquitous today where researchers and research are produced. First, money. The Germans realized that scholars have a hard time living on coin collected from callow, broke, and often drunk students. It's hard to write history books when you have to run a collection agency on the side. And, besides, most bookish types lack the muscle to collect anything but term papers. So the Germans, believing that it was important to fund teaching and research (an odd and novel thought in itself), made professors a line item in the government budget. Not a big line item, but a line item nonetheless. Second, freedom. Despite their mania for discipline, the Germans told scholars to do pretty much as they pleased and that they probably wouldn't be fired if they did it. Since most of these scholars were Germans themselves, *Ordnung* ensued. Finally, facilities. In the natural sciences, this meant laboratories. In the humanities and social sciences, this meant libraries. The Germans built a lot of them.

The entire system functioned as follows and still does (with exceptions noted below). The state hired and paid scholars to conduct research, the aim of which was to find out new things. The scholars, realizing that there is often a lot of grunt work to be done in research, hired and paid students (we would call them "graduate students") to help out and perhaps learn something in the process. The taking of students had the added benefit of ensuring that there would be more scholars in the future, which the state liked, and that the work of particular scholars would continue after they were no more, something the particular scholars liked. The output, so to speak, of the research university was new things and more scholars.

It worked. For in the late nineteenth and early twentieth centuries—that is, before the Nazis messed things up—the German research universities pumped out a lot of top-notch scholarly product. In physics: Max Planck, Albert Einstein, Erwin Schrodinger. In math: David Hilbert, Hermann Minkowski, Hermann Weyl. In biology: Rudolph Virchow, Robert Koch, Paul Ehrlich. In chemistry: Adolf von Baeyer, Hermann Emil Fischer, Fritz Haber. In the social sciences: Max Weber, Georg Simmel, Ferdinand Tonnies. In philosophy: Gottlob Frege, Friedrich Nietzsche, Edmund Husserl. Between 1901 and 1938, Germany won the Nobel Prize 38 times, more than any other country and over twice as often as the United States.

Naturally government officials, captains of industry, and university presidents in the Americas and elsewhere were watching. They knew just what to do: what the Germans were doing. The founders of a new university—Johns Hopkins, launched in 1876—were the first to introduce the German model into American higher education. Over the next several decades, many other American universities followed. It should be said that these American educational reformers did not slavishly impose the German model, but rather adapted it to peculiar American educational traditions, notably private funding and a focus on undergraduate education. In any case, the German model and variations thereupon were ubiquitous in the United States by the beginning of World War II. Again, it worked. The list of famous American scientists and scholars is too long to recite. Suffice it to say that beginning around 1950, the United States dominated the Nobel Prizes and continues to do so to this day.

Before the German model, history was not so much an

organized discipline as a hobby, primarily for wealthy people who knew a bit of Greek or Latin and enjoyed writing about the Classical World. Occasionally these gentlemen historians would be called "professors" and hold appointments (often unpaid) at universities or academies. Edward Gibbon, of *The History of the Decline and Fall of the Roman Empire* fame, is an excellent example. For the most part, however, these proto-historians were what we would call "amateurs" with no special training, no "research focus," and little interest beyond a fascination with history. Their purpose, insofar as they had one, was to provide "lessons" to their readers, who were overwhelmingly people just like them—wealthy, male, and fascinated by ancient Greece and Rome. They wrote books, and some of them we would call "history books," but they were quite different in content and form from modern history books. By our "professional" lights, these books usually rest on insufficient research, cover too much ground, and lack a well-formed "scholarly apparatus." Were Gibbon alive today, and were he to propose to his dissertation advisor a project on the decline and fall of the Roman Empire, he'd be thought insane. Were he to proceed with the project and finish it, no dissertation committee would ever accept his offering. And were he to try to get it published at a university press, he'd receive a short though courteous rejection letter. Poor Gibbon!

The man most often credited with introducing the German model into history was of course a German, namely Leopold von Ranke (no relation to Elizabeth). He was a bit like Gibbon and the gentlemen historians in that his passion was Classical Antiquity. He was different from them in that he had solid philological training, a good Lutheran's passion for going back to the original sources, and a half-formed idea that history could be made into a kind of empirical science. Happily for him (and us), his betters in the Prussian government and universities were enthused about making disciplines into empirical sciences, and they were glad to let him try to do so with history. Many of the distinctive characteristics of modern history research and writing can be traced to him, his colleagues, and his students or admirers: the concentration on primary and especially archival sources; the research seminar as a forum for investigation of those sources; the use of extensive footnotes and bibliographies in the writing up of results; the publication of these results in critical history journals and books; and, perhaps most importantly for us, the notion that history is a scientific discipline and, therefore, that historians must proceed through formal training and be certified as professionals.

Ranke's vision of scientific history was brought to the United States by one Herbert Baxter Adams. Adams was a member of the Establishment: he was born of old New England stock, attended Phillips Exeter Academy, and then proceeded to Amherst College. He was not, however, a backward-looking fellow. He knew the future was in Germany (where else?) and, a year after his graduation from Amherst, he went there to find it. In 1874 he took himself to Heidelberg and, together with 41 other American students, matriculated at the university to study nothing in particular. After a time, he travelled to Berlin and enrolled at the Friedrich-Wilhelm University. Then, after another time, he went back to Heidelberg where he received his doctorate in 1876.

Before bringing young Adams back to the United States to found the discipline Elizabeth wants to enter, we might well pause to note three items of interest, all of which show the distance between the German model as then practiced and modern history. First, it took Adams less than two years of intermittent study to get a *doctorate*. Granting that a German doctorate is not quite the same as an American doctorate, that's still remarkably fast. The average "time to degree" for American graduate students in history is currently over eight years (when they finish at all). Second, Adams didn't have to write *anything* to get that doctorate. He took a two-hour oral exam. That was it. I wouldn't advise you to tell that to an American graduate student struggling to finish a 500-page dissertation. Finally, Adams' doctorate was not in *history*. His major examination field was political science.

While in Heidelberg, Adams had heard about a new university in Baltimore, the aforementioned Johns Hopkins, that offered fellowships to support research. He wrote the president and trustees asking for a spot in history upon his return. "It is my aim to become a professor of historical and political science," he said. So great was the prestige of his German degree that Adams got the job, despite the fact that he had never written any history or political science at all. He went on to start or help start what was, arguably, the first history seminar (or "seminary," as it was called), the first modern history graduate program, the first history journal, and the first professional organization of historians inspired by the German model in the United States. By the beginning of World War I, Adams and his cohort had convinced pretty much every university president and historian in the United States that history was a science and historians were scientists. History was no longer a rich-man's hobby; it was a profession with its own rules and regulations, institutions and governing bodies, standards and practices.

Not long after the historical profession began to produce professional historians, professional historians began to produce professional history books. Interestingly, the two events were not exactly coterminous. Recall that Adams, certainly a professional historian when he returned from Heidelberg, had neither conceived nor completed any book, historical or otherwise. He was not unusual in this regard. For the first two generations of university-trained, doctorate-holding, professional historians, writing a book was neither a requirement nor expectation. It was assumed that, having conducted a major piece of research in the dissertation (though Adams didn't even do that), one would publish one or more articles in journals. Most historians pursuing academic careers did just that.

Nevertheless, some professional historians recognized that they could write books (the gentlemen historians did), perhaps should write books (the gentlemen historians thought so), and that there should be some mechanism for them to do so (such as the gentlemen historians had). It is in this realization that we discover the headwaters of the institution that is the modern university press. Truth be told, university presses *per se* are quite old. There was a press at Oxford University in 1478, another at Cambridge University in 1521, and, moving to the other side of the Atlantic, another at Harvard College in 1636. But these were really presses at universities, not university presses as we understand them. And since, as we've noted, universities were essentially religious institutions before the advent of the German model in the nineteenth century, their presses published exactly what you'd expect: the Holy Writ and titles that helped people read and understand the Holy Writ. Not exclusively, of course. The dons also deigned to issue the Greek and Roman classics, which dons everywhere then loved. By the seventeenth century, however, both the presses at Oxford and Cambridge were publishing some other sorts of things (and especially political pamphlets), though titles like *The Book of Common Prayer* and the works of Livy kept the candles lit.

Modern History—as opposed to Herodotus and such—came rather late to the presses at universities. The first so-called "history" published by Oxford University Press was a translation of Johannes Scheffer's *The History of Lapland* in 1674. Lapland! As even a cursory look makes clear, however, this book is not "history" at all, but rather an odd mishmash of observations on the Laps. Nonetheless, something approximating history books in our sense soon followed. For example, Oxford University Press published Earl Edward Hyde of Clarendon's *The History of the Rebellion and Civil Wars in England* in 1702. It was a hotly debated bestseller by the measure of the day, but, like Gibbon's *Decline and Fall*, it never would have made it out of the seminar room in ours.

Perhaps the press lowered its standards because Hyde had been the chancellor of Oxford University itself. Lore has it that the proceeds from *The History of the Rebellion* paid for the impressive Clarendon Building, the home of Oxford University Press (aka the "Clarendon Press") beginning in 1715. This is a pleasing story, but one doubts that any single history book ever made enough money to build anything but a hovel in central London.

Curiously, university presses did not publish the first modern history books. Not one of Ranke's books was published by a university press. Nor were those of Ranke's successors Johann Droysen, Heinrich Treitschke, and Theodor Mommsen. These historians—and there were many others like them in the nineteenth century—either didn't have the option of publishing with a university press or it didn't occur to them to do so. Not that university presses were eager to publish their books. The directors of these presses knew that it was easy to sell a new edition of the New Testament, while it was quite hard to sell a new history book on an old subject. They sensibly stuck to the low hanging fruit.

All that changed when the newly professionalized historians decided that every historian-in-the-making should produce a dissertation, which is to say a sort of history book—though not the real thing—that conveys the results of their arduous research. As we noted above, Adam's *Doktorvater* made no such demand when he took the PhD. This was a bit unusual, for the Germans were famous for producing obscure dissertations even then. Adams certainly knew this, and perhaps he felt that he'd missed an important step in his training. In any case, he and all his colleagues made sure that their doctoral students did not miss this step: they would require their protégés to write dissertations. So, as the German model spread, history dissertations began to pour forth from history departments in ever-greater numbers. The year Johns Hopkins opened its gates (1876), American universities produced exactly three history dissertations (all of them, incidentally, written at Harvard and about Anglo-Saxon law). That figure rapidly rose: in 1900—30 dissertation; in 1910—49 dissertations; in 1920—53 dissertations; in 1930—181 dissertations.

That's a lot of would-be history books. What to do with them? The thinking in the Ivory Tower was that they should be published as books. Historians like Adams thought so because both scholarship and the republic would benefit. University presidents like Daniel Coit Gilman, Adams' boss, thought so because they knew that books were a good way to sell the university to students and donors. The rub was that there was no market for obscure history books. The only people who would buy *A Foot in the Door: The History of Bulgarian Shoe Manufacturing from 1900 to 1905* were members of the Bulgarian Shoe Manufacturing Association (the "BSMA" to those in the trade)—and there weren't many of them. Therefore no commercial or "trade" publisher would touch a book like *A Foot in the Door* for it would mean a loss in the pocket.

If the likes of Adams and Gilman wanted to see that dissertations were published as books, they needed to find someone to buy them. They did—university libraries. Before our era, university libraries were pitiful places. They were generally small, poorly staffed, restricted to faculty, rarely open, and infrequently visited. The reason for this neglect is simple: neither scholars nor students really needed good libraries to do their work. What they needed was something like *The Harvard Classics*, aka, "Dr. Eliot's Five-Foot Shelf." That changed with the advent of the German model. In a research university, the library came to be seen as a kind of laboratory for the Liberal Arts, a place where investigations were undertaken, discoveries were made, and books were written. Naturally the new "research libraries," as they were called, needed to be big. Status-seeking universities entered into a kind of bibliographic arms race. They built ever-larger collections and ever-grander structures to house them.

Millions were spent when millions meant something.

Adams and Gilman recognized that the new super libraries would supply the demand necessary to print dissertations-become-books. All they needed now was someone to supply the supply. Trade publishers wouldn't do. If they published a university's books they would essentially deprive said university of both profit and publicity. If, however, a university published its own books—as had Oxford and Cambridge for so many centuries—then it would reap all the monetary and public relations benefits thereof. The course was clear. Cornell University Press opened in 1869, though its purpose was as much to train journalism students as to publish scholarly books. It closed in 1884 and did not reopen until 1930. Johns Hopkins launched its press in 1878; that press has been in continuous operation since. Thereafter, many universities opened their own presses in rapid succession: Chicago in 1891, California and Columbia in 1893, Toronto in 1901, Princeton in 1905, and so on. Today there are well over 100 university presses in North America.

With the advent of the university press, a new system of scholarly production and communications emerged, one that is with us even today. In it, universities fund research by their faculty members; they then fund the publication of that research by their university presses; and, finally, they fund the purchase of that published research by their own super libraries. The most peculiar thing about this system is that it does not take into account what readers—academic or otherwise—might want. It is supply driven, not demand driven. The result, as the head of Harvard's Widener Library noted in 1917, was a library full of books no one ever reads.

The numerous university presses which have started during the past thirty years are supported largely by the libraries. A considerable proportion of them entered the publishing business because it is well-known that a sufficient number of libraries can be relied on to buy anything that is issued under respectable auspices. They are kept going by the larger number of librarians, who are unable if they once secure a volume in a series, to refuse to purchase whatever else comes out in the same form. The result has been that a great many things have been printed for which there never was any demand either from readers or investigators of anything except academic statistics.

Harvard's head librarian suggested that university libraries stop buying everything university presses published and pay more attention to what readers actually wanted to read. But in the end the "investigators of academic statistics" won the day: having a huge library filled with university press books meant status, and in academia status trumps almost every other consideration.

This, then, is the machine that makes modern historians and history books: the German model research university, the seminar-based graduate program, the writing of dissertations, the desire to make dissertations into books, and the university library and press. The machine is remarkably productive: American history departments today produce around 1,000 dissertation-carrying professional historians annually; university presses publish something on the order of 12,000 titles, historical and otherwise, each year; the standard of scholarship represented in those dissertations and books is very high.

Yet there are problems. Only about half of those dissertation-carrying professional historians ever get jobs in history departments. History may have the poorest placement rate of any profession in the United States. Well aware of this sobering fact, Elizabeth's parents think that she should consider law school. Only a few people will ever have access to the 12,000 titles produced annually by university presses, and nearly all of them look quite a bit like the people who wrote the titles in question.

Elizabeth, idealist that she is, wants to spread the light of learning to ensure the prosperity of the republic. She's going to have a hard time doing it by writing history books and publishing them with university presses. Finally, the very standards of scholarship that distinguish modern history books from items like Gibbon's *Decline and Fall* have narrowed what a history book can be about to the point that, well, they are about nothing of public interest at all. *A Foot in the Door: The History of Bulgarian Shoe Manufacturing from 1900 to 1905* (Big Name University Press, 2010) may be "a path-breaking contribution to the study of *fin de siècle* Eastern European footwear," but it's not likely to be a contribution to anything else. Even Elizabeth, history major that she is, cannot muster a mustard seed of interest in Bulgarian shoes, *debut de siècle* or *fin de siècle*. If she's going to prosper in graduate school, that better change.

And it is to graduate school that Elizabeth will go. But before we take her there we would do well to discuss, if only briefly, another kind of history book, namely the popular kind. It may seem at first glance that the popular history book and the academic history book are two very different things. The former is often written by someone without a PhD in history; the latter is always written by someone with a PhD in history. The former is almost never a revision of a dissertation; the latter is often a revision of a dissertation. The former is usually published by a trade press or at least a university press acting like a trade press; the latter is always published by a university press acting like a university press. The former will be about something with name recognition, Cleopatra, the Civil War, or Watergate; the latter will not. The former will be heavily marketed and reasonably priced; the latter will be marketed not at all and will be expensive. The former will be read by a large number of people, most of whom are history buffs; the latter will be read by a small number of people, most of whom are professional historians and their students. The former will generate cash royalties for the author;

the latter will generate a job and perhaps tenure for the author. In sum, the popular history book is a commodity explicitly designed by its author and editor to sell in the marketplace for books. The academic history book, though it looks a lot like a commodity, is actually a credential designed by its author and her colleagues to advance a career. That's a big difference, and one should always keep it in mind when reading a history book, popular or academic.

At a certain point, however, the distinction between the two types collapses for a simple reason: nearly all popular history books are based in whole or part on academic history books and articles. The authors of popular history books are with rare exceptions college graduates, and often college graduates from elite universities. At these places, they doubtless learned the basics of the German model of historical research, particularly the difference between "primary sources"—usually documents from the time and place being studied—and "secondary sources"—contemporary writings about those times and places. For the most part, popular history writers neither have the time nor inclination to delve into the primary sources for any but illus-trative purposes. Their mission—to tell a true story about the past that will sell—can be accomplished with heavy reliance on secondary sources, especially academic history articles and books. Some may go to archives, and most will read published primary sources. They will all cite and quote primary material. Nonetheless, they will build the entire frame and much of the detail of their true stories about the past on the work of academic historians.

Enough about popular history books. Elizabeth knows that, as a rule, academic historians poo-poo them because they are written for the market rather than for the ages. She, hoping to join the confraternity of tenured historians, has no intention of writing one. She wants to write an academic history book. She's about to take a big step in that direction.

Chapter 2

Training a History-Book Writer

There's really only one time in a person's life in which you can easily convince him to die for his country or go to graduate school in history—at about 22 years of age.
—Reinhardt Friedrich Freiherr von Teufel

Elizabeth Ranke, now BA, knew she was going to graduate school before she entered Twiddletwaddle College. Her parents both have graduate degrees and she believes (with some justification) that a graduate degree is more or less necessary for a "good" career. The choice of the humanities came in her junior year. She was a fair science and math student, though she took only the required classes, which were few. Those subjects, however, did not capture her imagination. Moreover, she learned from her pre-med friends that careers in the STEM ("Science, Technology, Engineering and Math") disciplines are rather rough going, particularly for women. Not to put too fine a point on it, the culture of these fields is very competitive and often macho— the result, perhaps, of many decades of domination by competitive, macho men. They are all about "big results." In the STEM trades, size matters. As for the social sciences, Elizabeth did very well in all of those but they didn't light her fire either. Most of them were just too much like the "real" sciences, overstuffed with variables, data sets, correlations, regressions, models, tests and so on. She took an American literature class in which the professor assigned WH Auden's snotty poem "Under Which Lyre," which includes the following advice for college students:

Thou shalt not answer questionnaires
Or quizzes upon World-Affairs

Nor with compliance
Take any test. Thou shalt not sit
With statisticians nor commit
A social science

Elizabeth won't.

The humanities, Elizabeth knows, are different than the sciences, "real" and otherwise. They are much more, well, humane, not to mention gender-balanced. The historians, literary scholars, and writers of "serious fiction" whom she admires are all well-mannered, well-spoken, and well-intentioned folks. They really care about words and how to put them together. They read all things New York: *The New York Times*, *The New Yorker*, and *The New York Review of Books*. If they are lucky, they've published in one of them; if not, they aspire to. They are all concerned about social justice, civil rights, and religious fundamentalism. They vote Democratic. In other words, they are a lot like her father.

Moreover, humanists seem to have great gigs. Elizabeth's father says that the ditch-digging in academic careers in the humanities is all front-loaded. You have to work hard in high school, college, and graduate school. Then, when and if you are lucky enough to land a tenure-track job, you have to put in long hours turning your dissertation into a book. You need to watch your teaching and committee work because you know the deans will. But if you've done those things, you'll be granted tenure and the load will lighten appreciably. You're not even 40 and you have a reasonably well-paying, permanent job for life. If you want to continue your research, you can. If you want to devote long hours to teaching, you can. If you want to move up the administrative ladder, you can. But you don't have to do any of these things. You are—to use an unkind though not entirely inaccurate analogy—a "made man" (or woman, as the case may be).

This isn't to say, of course, that the day after being granted tenure humanists put their feet up on their desks, turn on NPR, and relax. They don't. The professional ambitions and work habits that get them through the hard part die hard. Elizabeth's father is a recovering workaholic. She remembers that when she was growing up he was usually in the office or wished he were. He was always writing some new paper or book. Since Elizabeth's mother threatened divorce, he's gotten better. He's not going to be a star and knows it, which makes him a bit sad. Nonetheless, he's got a prestigious, relatively cushy job that he can't lose unless he does something really stupid like grope an undergraduate. He's not going to do that; he's got too much to lose and knows it.

So the humanities it is for Elizabeth. But which one? She loves to read, but that doesn't really help because all the humanities are really about reading. She loves to write, but the same applies. In the end, it was nothing to do with the nature of specific humanities disciplines that determined her course, but rather something about Elizabeth's politics. When Elizabeth's mother had been in college in the early 1970s, she'd been a member of a radical feminist group, the "Women's Liberation Army." More specifically, Elizabeth's mom had been the editor of the WLA newspaper, *The Gender Front*, and, luckily for Elizabeth, she had the entire run of issues. They fascinated Elizabeth. Though she considered herself a feminist—who didn't?—it was hard to understand what she read in *The Gender Front*. How could not shaving your legs or not wearing a bra be a liberating act? To answer these questions she took several classes from a well-known women's historian, professor Jean Sexton. She was brilliant, eloquent, and still politically engaged. Her articles and books were terrific. Elizabeth was hooked. Professor Sexton became her advisor and honors-thesis director.

Elizabeth believed that she had to get into a top-ten graduate program. Professor Sexton told her that it was difficult to land a "good" tenure-track history job in general, and nearly impossible for graduates of lessor history programs. She recalled hearing one of her own mentors in graduate school say that all he needed to fill an open slot in the department was a list of recent PhDs from the "best" history department in the United States. Of course, Professor Sexton admitted, this was unfair and regrettable. But, like it or not, status matters a lot in academic hiring, particularly in disciplines like history where quality is very difficult to measure objectively. If Elizabeth failed to get into a top-tier program, Professor Sexton suggested, then perhaps she should follow her parents' counsel and consider law school.

All this advice did was steel Elizabeth's resolve to get into a "good" graduate school. Happily, she was both an excellent student and she had a lot of help. Having grown up in an academic family, she knew the ropes of an academic career—what it required, how it proceeded, what to expect from it. Academia is an odd place and it really helps to know your way around it before you go wandering into it. Elizabeth had a map. Moreover, she was about to graduate from a "good" school. Honestly, she didn't think she'd learned much—or at least much of value—while at Twiddletwaddle. But she knew that the very fact that she'd gotten in and through signaled something about her to admissions committees. It could hardly hurt that many of the people who would review her application were probably Twiddletwaddle alums; nor did it hurt that her recommenders at Twiddletwaddle personally knew members of the admissions committee. She's reminded of something a cynical professor of hers once quipped: "It's not a small world. It's a large, well-stratified world that gives the appearance of being small." Again, regrettable but true.

Professor Sexton explained how to apply. First Elizabeth needed to pick target schools. To make this decision, she should look through the publications of faculty members at top-tier programs. By this point, Elizabeth would probably be able to identify particular scholars she would like to work with. She wouldn't find them in every program, but since gender history or women's history were sufficiently popular subspecialties, she would find a few at several of them. Elizabeth would apply to these schools, in addition to one or two lower-ranked safety schools that would doubtless admit her and would, therefore, give her the option of attending if law school began to look less attractive. The application forms were simple enough: name, rank, serial number. Only a few things remained. Transcripts. Elizabeth's grades are quite good, so no trouble there. Letters of recommendation. Elizabeth is well liked by several professors, so no trouble there. And, finally, a statement of purpose and writing sample. These sound like two things, but Professor Sexton explained that they should be intertwined. The statement of purpose should lay out with some specificity what Elizabeth planned to study. "I want to study history, write about it, and teach it for the good of humankind" will not do. Rather, one has to describe a research program on X, where X is something narrow that the student has already written on and someone in the target department might be interested in. For Elizabeth, this is simple. She wants to study radical feminist groups at American colleges in the 1960s. She has written a senior thesis on the topic—that's her writing sample. And she knows that several scholars in her target departments might well be interested in supervising such work. Elizabeth is done.

Elizabeth's advisor is not. Professor Sexton is very fond of Elizabeth and thinks she would make a terrific historian. She wants to do everything possible to help her find a place in a "good" graduate program. She's guided Elizabeth through the application process and she's written her a terrific letter of recommendation. Now she will "reach out," that is, contact key colleagues at Elizabeth's target institutions to tell them what a great candidate she is. This used to be called "picking up the phone," but now most of it's done over e-mail.

—Original Message—
From: Jean Sexton [mailto:
jeansexton@prestigiouscollege.edu]
Sent: Friday, December 17, 2011 9:22 AM
To: Barfield, Sarah
Subject: Elizabeth Ranke

Hi Sarah,

It was good to see you at the convention. Too bad there
wasn't a bar at the reception, because I sure could have used
a drink. Maybe next year? Aren't you on the coordinating
committee? Make it happen!

In any case, I'm writing about a student of mine, Elizabeth
Ranke. She's applied to your program (I wrote for her, as
you'll see). I think she's just terrific. Her work on radical
feminist groups in the '60s is right down your alley. IMHO,
you'd be wise to take her and lucky to get her.

Have a good break!

Best, JS

_____

Each year, top-ranked history programs get hundreds of serious
applications from serious candidates. The committees that must
decide whom to admit and under what terms, therefore, have a
very difficult job. "Reaching out" helps them do it for two
reasons. First, it sometimes gives them additional information
about the candidate. Second, it's an opportunity to trade favors.
Once again, regrettable but true.

Elizabeth's fate is now in the hands of several graduate admissions committees. These are composed of department members,

mostly senior, from a variety of subdisciplines. They get the applications and review them. Because there are so many, they sometimes scan them for what might be called "key indicators." The three most important are research focus, college, and grade-point average. The first is used to throw out candidates who could never find advisors in the department. If a candidate wants to study sixteenth-century German religious sects and there is no one in the department who does anything even close, they get thrown out of the pile. College is important for all the reasons we've already mentioned. It is usually used for preliminary ranking within fields, the graduates of the more prestigious colleges being placed above those from less prestigious ones. Grade-point average is used in the same way: the higher the average, the higher the rank. Interestingly, most history departments pay no attention to standardized tests unless they indicate an applicant has a poor command of English. A bad score on the language portion of a standardized test—be it the GRE or TOEFL—will almost certainly get a candidate thrown out of the pile. Elizabeth has a potential advisor, went to a "good school," has excellent grades, and did well on the GRE, so she makes it through.

Two other "key indicators," though of a very different sort, are race and gender. Every American university has a policy that forbids discrimination on the base of race, gender, and a host of other things. Every American university also has something like an "Equal Opportunity and Diversity Office" (EODO) that makes sure everyone complies with that policy. And though the EODO does not usually meddle in graduate admissions, the principle behind it—namely, that the institution will not allow bias in recruitment except when it has the opportunity to rectify existing underrepresentation—pervades the academy in general and history departments in particular. The committee members want to see a balance of genders and proper representation of racial minorities in admissions, and they know the entire department feels the same way. If there are too many Xs and not enough Ys at any stage in the process, then department members may raise questions. For this reason, the committee will balance and re-balance their lists as they are winnowed from very long to long to short. Of course this balancing and re-balancing *is* discrimination on the base of race and gender, but no matter. Elizabeth is white, which is not to her advantage. But she is female, and that helps a little. She'll be fine.

Once this preliminary sorting ends, the hard work begins. It involves matching, ranking, and horse-trading. Matching means placing candidates with potential advisors. In some cases, committee members will send applications to these people to see if they might be keen to take them on. The committee takes what potential advisors say about a candidate very seriously. Elizabeth's potential advisor, Sarah Barfield, likes what she sees. Ranking means placing the entire pool in some order and, within it, aspirants to particular subdisciplines in some order. This can be tricky, because a candidate might rank high in the entire pool but relatively low in a subdiscipline. Elizabeth's case is the opposite: she doesn't rank very highly in the entire pool, but in women's history she's near the top. Horse-trading means different committee members representing different interests in the department—women's history, Ancient history, German history, you name it—negotiate the final composition of the pool so that every such interest is fairly represented. Since the women's history faction in Barfield's department only wants three admissions—one of whom is Elizabeth—it needn't go begging any other factions for additional spots.

But Elizabeth is not in yet. The list of admissions still has to go before the entire department. Ordinarily, no objections will be voiced; most faculty members have neither the time nor incli-nation to battle their colleagues over admissions decisions. They consider it best—and certainly most politic—just to trust the committee did its work well. The principal exception here is when the committee presents a list of admissions with a significant gender imbalance or without a sufficient number of underrepresented minorities. Too many of these or those will cause a lot of handwringing and perhaps even some raised voices. The list may have to be re-balanced once more. And Elizabeth, being white, could get thrown out at the last minute for this reason. As it happens, though, all is in gender and racial order. She makes it through once more.

Elizabeth is now sure to receive a "We are pleased to inform you..." letter. Just what will be in it, though, may not have been determined at this stage, for there remains the matter of a "package." A package is a set of emoluments that will determine how an incoming graduate student will pay for graduate school. At some elite and very well-endowed American universities, a "full ride" package comes with admissions: if you get in, then they will pay for you to live and study for a certain number of years. At less wealthy universities, a "full ride" package will be offered to the very best students in the hopes of attracting them from the aforementioned very well-endowed institutions. But at most universities and for most students, a package is a mix of things that make graduate study just barely possible. It might include a "tuition-fee waiver," subsidized housing, and perhaps even a very modest stipend.

It will almost always include teaching. Most professors at research universities would much rather do research than teach undergraduates, though you will never hear them admit it. Research is both rewarding and rewarded, with status if nothing else; undergraduate teaching is neither terribly rewarding nor rewarded. It's not that most research professors despise teaching. They don't. It's just that after you've given that same lecture on the *sans-culottes* in the French Revolution for the ninth time in as many years, you get tired of the *sans-culottes* in the French Revolution. Academics often get wound up, but they are not wind-up toys. It's fortunate, then, that professors at research universities have a bunch of enthusiastic would-be historians around who can take over their teaching job in part or whole. That they get "experience in the classroom" is an added bonus from a pedagogical point of view. That they are not paid very much is an added bonus from the economic point of view. Everybody wins, except perhaps the undergraduates who expected that they would be taught by professors. But they really have no say in the matter despite the fact that they are periodically asked about the quality of the instruction they receive.

Once Elizabeth has received responses from all the programs to which she applied, she needs to decide where she is going to go. In cases like Elizabeth's this is usually not difficult: she simply chooses the "best" program with someone she can work with in it. Here "best" means "with the highest status among people who might eventually hire you." Naturally Elizabeth knows that this "best" is not to be confused with the "best" in any objective sense; after all, her father is as good as anyone in his field and he doesn't teach at a big name school. But she knows status matters, especially in soft disciplines where it's hard to tell whose result is bigger than whose. The nature of her package is not terribly important: unless the school offers her nothing at all (which is highly unlikely, because Elizabeth is a very good prospect), her family is wealthy enough to support her at least for a time. Elizabeth's parents know what the parents of less-academically experienced prospects do not, namely that she can get both grants and teaching after she arrives. An in-person plea to her advisor, whomever that might be, can go a long way toward getting funding. And if it doesn't work out, it doesn't work out. There's always law school.

In the event, Elizabeth decides to go to Hornblower University because its history program is ranked fourth in the nation, the eminent women's historian Sarah Barfield teaches there, and they offered her a fair package. She's sad she wasn't accepted by a higher ranked program; there were some tears. Hornblower, however, will do fine. Happily, it is not located in the South or the Midwest—not that she thinks there's anything wrong with those places, it's just she doesn't want to live there, at least not at this point in her life.

So young Elizabeth is off to storied Hornblower to study the history of feminism and write a history book about the same. Before she does either of these things, however, there are preliminaries to be attended to. She will need to take a number of seminars. Big history departments are ordinarily divided along regional and temporal lines. As for regions, the most capacious and common divisions are American, European, and World, though a really big history department might have African, Latin American and South Asian as well. In most history programs in the United States, around 50% of the permanent faculty are Americanists, 25% Europeanists, and 25% something else. These broad geographic categories are themselves divided into national subdivisions: American history, German history, French history, Indian history, Chinese history and so on. Most historians identify with one of these national categories: "I'm an American historian," "I'm a German historian," "I'm a French historian." As for time period, typical divisions include Ancient, Medieval, Early Modern, and Modern. In most history programs in the United States, something on the order of 75% of permanent faculty study the modern period. Again, there are finer distinctions, and they tend to become finer still as one moves forward in time. As a general rule, the older the stuff a historian studies, the more time a historian has to cover. Ancient historians are responsible for many centuries; a modern American historian might be responsible for a few decades.

Obviously this "distribution of attention," so to say, is biased in favor of contemporary America and Europe. The United States, with less than 300 years of history and around 300 million people, might get the exclusive regard of ten historians in a big department; India, with 3,000 years of history and well over a billion people might get the attention of one. Without going into the reasons for this bias, suffice it to say, it could be much worse. Before the later nineteenth century, the Ancient World and the United States were practically the only historical subjects taught in American colleges and universities. In much of the world even today, national history completely dominates the history curriculum. Elizabeth has the option of studying, say, Russian history at Hornblower; her counterpart in Russia probably doesn't have the option of studying American history, at least very thoroughly.

There has long been another way to organize the historical discipline, namely, along thematic lines. Ranke, whom we've met before, wrote among other things diplomatic history, not just early modern and modern German history. His near contemporary, Fredric William Maitland, wrote legal history, not just medieval and early modern English history. And yet another historian of Ranke's generation, Jacob Burckhardt, wrote cultural history, not just the history of Renaissance Italy. As a rule, these thematic histories are not explicitly represented in modern American history departments: most faculties do not have resident diplomatic historians, legal historians, or cultural historians the way they have resident colonial-era American, early modern German, or modern Chinese historians. And though the temporal-national scheme reigns, for some decades now it has been challenged by what might be called the "new thematic history." Interestingly, its origins are not to be found in the "old thematic history," but rather in modern politics, and more specifically in a number of political movements that have sprung up over the course of the last century.

The first of these was the labor movement. Marx wrote that all history was the history of class struggle, though he only sketched a bit of all history. It fell to Marxist historians to fill in the blanks and, beginning in the later nineteenth century, they did just that. As sympathy for socialism spread in Europe, so did the practice of writing working-class history. Most Americans rejected socialism, but in the later 1950s and 1960s a group of left-leaning American academics began to express sympathy for persecuted socialists and some socialist causes, if not for socialism itself. Like European Marxists, American "New Left" historians were very concerned about the exploitation of the working class by greedy capitalists. Unlike European Marxists, they were not Marxists, so they avoided party jargon like "working-class history." Instead, they wrote "labor history," and do so to this day.

The invention of labor history inspired other politically-engaged American scholars—all left-leaning—to promote other sorts of thematic history. The most famous and successful examples are African-American history, Native-American history, and women's history; every sizable history department will have specialists in these three thematic fields. More recently, queer history, disability history, and genocide history have been added to the mix. Thematic history is not focused exclusively on groups of people; historians worried about the destruction of the environment have of late launched environmental history, now a major subfield.

Elizabeth knows enough about these modes of classification to be aware that she is a women's historian in training. Her program, however, will require her to learn more than women's history. Most departments have distribution requirements, meaning that they make PhD candidates learn about times and places beyond their research interest. The distribution require-ments are met by choosing, say, three historical subspecialties (called "fields"), taking seminars in those fields, and then passing a comprehensive examination (called "comps") covering the material presented in those seminars. In most departments, candidates can choose whatever fields they want. Elizabeth could select, for example, modern America as her main field, Africa as her second field, and ancient China as her third field. But she won't do that. As a rule, history departments promote rapid specialization, meaning that they tell graduate students to adopt comps fields close to their main field. In Elizabeth's case, this means that she will probably only take seminars touching on American history, and mostly modern American history.

What happens in these seminars? The ideal, according to the nineteenth-century advocates of the German model, is that a seminar should be a lab for the soft sciences, a place where professors and advanced students do primary research. The typical graduate history seminar never approaches this ideal, with some rare exceptions. In modern history seminars, graduate students read history books and articles. A lot of them. This is why the most frequent title given to graduate history seminars is "Readings in X History," where X is some subdiscipline. Sometimes professors will provide the students with a reading list; sometimes professors will leave it to the students to decide what to read so long as it's in the field under study.

In either case, the aim of all this reading is not so much to learn a bit of history, but rather to get a firm grasp of what other historians have said about that bit of history. As we saw in Chapter 1, the introduction of the German model, the idea that every historian should publish a book, and the creation of university presses to publish those books led to a flood of new historical work. "The literature," as it is called in the trade, expanded mightily. As it did, novice historians like Elizabeth were presented with a problem that Ranke never could have imagined: too many history books and articles. It is no easy task to read the bulk of the literature on even relatively minor fields like early modern Russian history; it is impossible in fields like modern American history. There's just too much stuff. Since no one can read it all, the only choice is to sample what's on offer. And that is precisely what happens in most graduate seminars: a little of this, a bit of that, and some of the other thing. Professors do not, of course, sample the literature at random. Rather, they assign a catalogue of "greatest hits" comprising items their advisors assigned to them so many years ago, albeit with a few new additions. Since history professors tend to be an idiosyncratic bunch and the literature is so enormous, no two "Readings in X" seminars are going to be exactly alike. In most cases, they will be strikingly different even though they are nominally about the same thing.

In addition to reading, there will be a lot of talking in a graduate history seminar. In most seminars, students discuss the books they've read that week. In some cases, they will all have read the same books and the professor will serve as the inquisitor. In other cases, they will all have read different books and each student will give a summary and respond to questions from the field. The tenor of these discussions is generally quite staid; everyone speaks in measured tones, is respectful of others, and well-versed in the material. There is no over-talking, no yelling, no insulting. And though these courtly parlays are usually apolitical, they are very politically correct. Irony, satire, and most humor are largely banished. This is not because the professor imposes a speech code on the students; rather, it's because the students—being successful, bright, overwhelmingly liberal graduates of "good" schools—have mastered the code themselves. To put it briefly, graduate seminars in history are no fun at all.

In addition to talking, there may be some writing. Some professors—particularly older ones trained in Europe—do not require students to write papers in graduate seminars; the readings and discussions are deemed sufficient. Most, however, do assign papers. The ostensible purpose of these writing assignments is twofold: to teach the students how to write in the style of academic history, and to help them begin to write articles that might just be published some day in another form.

Given the first purpose, it may come as a surprise to learn that most history professors do not really try to teach their graduate students how to write. They will pay reasonably close attention to technical matters: spelling, transliteration, citation formatting, making bibliographies. These are easy enough to check, and every seasoned historian knows the rules of formatting and such by heart. But as to the construction of sentences, paragraphs, sections, and entire articles—what used to be called "composition"—they have nothing to say beyond "well written" or "needs work." Again, they do not neglect the finer point of literary style because they are evil; rather, they disregard it because they either do not understand it or do not have the time to teach it. It is for this reason that the prose in the vast majority of history books is mechanical: it reads like it was written by a contraption with a very limited, entirely invariant set of lexical, syntactical, grammatical, and organizational rules. In this sense, the dry, distant, analytic, politically-correct style of the seminar discussion is recapitulated in the seminar paper, and later in published journal articles and history books. On the one hand, this might not be a bad thing, for such a style takes the author out of the frame and focuses the reader's attention on the subject under consideration. On the other hand, it makes most modern history writing rather lifeless.

The second purpose of the paper is, as we've said, to start students on the road to publication. And here professors can be very valuable, for they know all about what is publishable and how to publish it. Generally speaking, a publishable historical article or book is one that addresses a "known problem." If an author writes about something that is either unknown (which is to say of interest to no one) or not a problem (which is to say something that has been gone over so many times as to be old hat), it will never be published. One must follow, then, a historical variation on the Goldilocks principle in selecting a historical topic to write about: it can't be too obscure, it can't be too well-known, it must be "just right." Most experienced historians know the parameters of this marginal zone very well, and they will guide seminar attendees to stay well within it. The downside to this mode of picking problems is that unknown topics remain unknown and well-trodden topics are not frequently revisited. But no matter—the safe and nearly universal play in the seminar paper writing (and, for that matter, in dissertation writing, article writing, and book writing) is to find a topic that is "just right."

In Elizabeth's seminar "Readings in Twentieth-Century American History," Professor Barfield assigned all the students— five women and two men—a book a week, together with some articles indented to survey the literature. As had her advisor before her, Professor Barfield selected classics in the various subdisciplines of modern American history—political history, economic history, social history, African-American history, labor history, and women's history. She added a book on queer history and Latino history, two relatively new fields. The discussions were serious and somewhat nerve-wracking. When it came time to choose a paper topic, Professor Barfield recommended that she select something related to her probable dissertation topic, that is, late twentieth-century American feminism. And though this topic hewed to the Goldilocks principle, it was still awfully large. To get a handle on it, Professor Barfield suggested that Elizabeth write a historiographical survey of the literature. Elizabeth agreed and she began to read book after book and article after article. Professor Barfield told her to try to identify particular schools of thought within the literature and to position herself within them. This proved very difficult, for the scholars who had written on the subject had not associated themselves with schools of thought. She did the best she could, dividing and subdividing the literature into ever more narrow categories. At a certain point she began to wonder whether she was creating—rather than discovering—schools of thought in the literature. But no matter. Professor Barfield liked the paper a lot, though she found numerous technical errors, particularly in the formatting of footnotes. She said Elizabeth's paper was well on the way to being a "valuable contribution to the field." It just needed "a little work."

During her three years of course work, Elizabeth not only learned the material she would need to pass her comps and wrote some papers that might one day be seen in print, she also gained a sense of her peers. She liked some of them and didn't like others. But more than anything else she came to understand that they were a discontented, competitive, tense bunch. Everyone complained about having too much work, and indeed many of her peers seemed to work 24 hours a day, day in and day out. These people did nothing but history. She thought their mindless devotion a bit odd, but it also occurred to her that these worka-holics might know something that she did not, namely, that it was this sort of near fanatical effort that was required to get a "good job" in history.

Elizabeth noted that there was a lot of discussion in the graduate lounge about "good jobs," or rather the lack of them. The most recent issue of the Historical Society of the United States' (HSUS) newsletter trumpeted the "excellent news" that "over 50%" of recent history PhDs found employment in history departments in the past year. That didn't seem like "excellent news" to her nor, she imagined, did it seem like "excellent news" to the 50% of recent history PhDs who were working temp jobs in office blocks. Of course HSUS also noted that many of those "who chose not to pursue the academic track" used the skills they'd acquired in history PhD programs to land excellent jobs in a whole variety of interesting fields. This seemed frighteningly out-of-touch to Elizabeth. She wanted to be a history professor and so did everyone else in her program; there was no talk of "choosing" not to pursue the academic track, though there was a lot of talk of being forced out of the profession for want of academic jobs. No one had any idea what the "marketable skills" mentioned by HSUS were—a detailed knowledge of medieval French chivalry?

It appeared to Elizabeth that things were not getting any better. The incoming graduate class in her program was larger than ever, meaning that the glut of historians on the academic job market would only grow. What were the professors on the admissions committees thinking when they admitted all these hopeful students, many of whom they knew would never get the academic jobs they so desperately wanted? She knew they were not thinking about preparing these candidates for jobs outside academia, because the department offered absolutely no guidance of this sort. It ran workshops on how to apply for academic jobs, how to interview for academic jobs, and how to negotiate academic jobs. But it paid no attention at all to making its graduates ready to find a job in the real world. Elizabeth suspected that this was either because most professors didn't care or, more likely, most professors had never worked in the real world and knew nothing about it. Almost all the history professors at Hornblower had gone from BA to MA to PhD to tenure-track jobs without a significant break. This being so, it would be hard for them to advise anyone on what sort of nonacademic work might be available for a PhD in history.

Elizabeth began to despair. She found herself Googling "law school application deadlines" and going to sites that promised easy "transitions out of academia." The fact that several students in her graduate cohort had already quit the program did not help one bit. She decided to discuss the issue with her advisor. Professor Barfield said she understood Elizabeth's anxiety; times were indeed tough for would-be historians. In fact, she said, they had been for decades. Nonetheless she encouraged Elizabeth to stick it out. In so doing she had several motives. First, Professor Barfield was genuinely concerned: Elizabeth was a bright young scholar who, given the opportunity, would doubtless make a "significant contribution to the field." Professor Barfield wanted the best for her. But she also realized that she, her department, and Hornblower itself had a real stake in seeing Elizabeth and others like her complete the program. After all, Professor Barfield had argued for increased graduate admissions, particularly in the area of women's history. She, like so many of her colleagues, wanted to build a big, prestigious program, one that would attract the best students. The department and deans had given her the resources to conduct this building project. But if Elizabeth and others like her abandoned the program, then it might raise questions about Professor Barfield's initiative. Her status might fall. The status of the department might fall. Indeed the status of the university itself might fall. Elizabeth had to stay.

She did, against the better judgment of her mother who once again suggested law school. Her advisor's pep talk lifted her spirits and gave her confidence that good things would come if she would just buckle down. "My students all get jobs," Professor Barfield said without elaborating. The most important factor in Elizabeth's decision, however, had nothing to do with getting a job or not. It had to do with the material she was studying. In a number of her seminars Elizabeth had returned to the topic she had studied in her senior thesis in college, the Women's Liberation Army. She searched for and found a host of primary sources that she had known nothing about when writing that thesis. These included feminist newspapers, manifestos, pamphlets, and even several caches of letters. The deeper she dug, the more she was hooked. Imperceptibly, her goal shifted from wanting to write a history book and become a professor to wanting to find out what happened and why. Reading the literature was a chore; trying to unravel the mystery of feminism on American college campuses in the 1960s was a treat, particularly when it involved immersing herself in the primary sources themselves. If she used her imagination, it seemed as if she was really *there*. This experience was intoxicating. None of it made any sense to her mother. She had actually been there and, upon reflection, found the entire episode more embarrassing than interesting. "Why," Elizabeth's mother asked, "are you so into this stuff?" Elizabeth paused and thought about how to answer. She really didn't know, but she wanted to find a way to make her mother understand. Then she hit upon it. "Mom, I'm just a history geek I guess." So she was, and so are most historians. For it's difficult to explain why they go through what they go through to become historians and be historians without recourse to willful suppression of personal interest in favor of blind devotion to understanding the past.

After passing her comps—a kind of quiz conducted by several professors on the literature—Elizabeth began work on her dissertation prospectus, a kind of plan for writing her PhD thesis. It went through many drafts over a period of ten months. She first proposed to write on the history of feminism in the Western World in the 1960s. Her advisor scotched that project, noting that it was too big and she didn't have the languages necessary. She then proposed to study the history of radical feminism in the Anglophone world in the 1960s. Again, too big, and besides she'd never taken any courses to speak of in the Anglophone world outside the United States. After that, she proposed to study the history of feminism in the United States in the 1960s. Sensible, but the topic still covered too much ground. A bit frustrated by this point, she then proposed to study radical feminism in American higher education in the 1960s. Closer, but still no cigar. Finally, she proposed to study radical feminist student groups in American higher education in the 1960s. This, her advisor said, might just be doable, but she had her doubts. After all, there are hundreds of colleges and universities in the United States. Was Elizabeth going to look in the archives of them all or even a selection of the most important? Clearly not at this stage in her career. The clock was ticking; her package was due to run out in three years; once it did money would become an issue.

So Professor Barfield suggested focusing on a single, large campus where feminists were particularly active in the period, namely, the University of Westcostia, Priestly. Though she wanted to write a big book, Elizabeth agreed. She wrote up the prospectus. In it, she sketched the subject, provided a provisional chapter-by-chapter plan, and identified archival primary sources, published primary sources, and the relevant literature. At the end of her fourth year in graduate school, she defends the prospectus before a group of four professors. They concurred that hers was a fine, workable project and send her on her way to do what she needed to do.

Chapter 3

Writing a History Book

Writing and publishing a history book is like performing your masterpiece at the Staatsoper to an empty hall.
—Reinhardt Friedrich Freiherr von Teufel

Elizabeth Ranke, now ABD ("All But Dissertation"), presently needs to research and write a history book, or at least a proto-history book. It's not at all clear to her, however, that her graduate training has taught her how to complete this task. She can quickly and efficiently find the literature on a historical topic. She can scan that literature at a remarkable pace. She can talk about it eloquently, politely, and with considerable understanding. She can teach it, or at least the little of it presented in undergraduate discussion sections. And she can write short essays summarizing and critiquing it. But research and write a book of, say, 400 pages? That's different. Of course she will have her advisor's help. Professor Barfield has told her to send her drafts of chapters as she finishes them. She'll critique them and sent them back for revision. Sounds good, Elizabeth thinks to herself, but how do I research and write those chapters? Where's the manual? Elizabeth begins to realize that she's going to have to teach herself how to write a history book. And, more frightening still, she's going to have to do much of the work alone in a place where she knows almost no one, that is, Priestly, Westcostia. It could be worse: one of her colleagues has to go to Bogota to do her research, and another to Kiev. Still, she doesn't cherish the thought of leaving all her friends.

She spends another two semesters at Hornblower "preparing." This involves reading more and more of the literature directly related to her subject, of the literature somewhat related to her subject, and of the literature seeming to have nothing to do with her subject. When asked why she's reading the complete works of the French philosophical guru Darridont, she says she's "engaging the theoretical literature." In actuality, she's just temporizing. She goes from "G4"—a graduate student in her fourth year—to "G5" with nothing much to show for it except a historically useless knowledge of esoteric French philosophical theory. Elizabeth's advisor has seen this before. Some of her students "engaged the literature" at Hornblower for years when they should have been reading primary sources and writing their always-about-to-be-submitted chapters. Their "packages" run dry and then they come begging to the department for additional support. Since all that support is going to the promising new crop of first-year graduate students and those still in the regular pipeline, there is nothing to give them. In other words, they become problems. Professor Barfield is not going to let Elizabeth go the way of the "G12." She calls her into the office and tells her to get to Westcostia, ASAP. There are some tears, but Elizabeth agrees this is what she must do.

She makes arrangements and heads off to Priestly. Her parents know some people there, and she stays in their spare bedroom until she finds an apartment. Eventually she rents a dingy, drab, overpriced affair that comes with two flat mates—a Chinese chemistry student who seems to speak little or no English and a latter-day hippie who works nights at an organic food co-op and smokes a lot of weed. The chemistry student is always in the lab, the hippie is always sleeping, and Elizabeth avoids the place whenever possible. She spends most of her time in one or another university or city archive. She tells her advisor by e-mail that she's found "amazing stuff," and she means it. The repositories contain a treasure trove of information on feminist student groups, their activities and publications, and official efforts to control them.

The only hitch, and it's a big one, is that the files are not terribly well indexed or organized. For the past two decades, Westcostia has been in deep fiscal trouble: too much money was going out and not enough coming in. State legislators were looking for places to cut spending, and the obvious—which is to say politically safest—options seemed to be universities and local "nonessential" services. These legislators knew that most voters don't really have a good grasp of what people at universities do. According to many elected officials, they don't do much of anything and, unlike almost everyone else, can't be fired for it. And things like archives? From the point of view of voters, they are "nonessential" services *par excellence*. Some officials wonder why the voters are paying for them at all. So, when the folks in the state house get their cleavers out, they know just where to go to cut expenses and win votes all at the same time.

Elizabeth knows that most people at universities—and professors in particular—work very hard, and she thinks archives contribute mightily to the commonweal. Nonetheless, the archives she's working in are something of a mess because they are understaffed. Again, it could be much worse: the archives in Bogota and Kiev are even more unorganized and, besides, they are closed most days. She finds herself not only having to learn how to write a history book, but also having to learn how to arrange an archive. In truth, the archival work is fun. Because the files are not well ordered, she never knows what she's going to find. When she spends hours and discovers nothing, that's dispiriting. But when she spends hours and happens upon some unexpected something, that's really encouraging. She begins to think of herself as a kind of historical prospector, dipping her pan in the stream of the archive, sifting the documentary stones, and, occasionally, coming up with some incredible nugget.

These she collects and, over time, something magical happens. They begin to sort themselves. First, chronologically, one after another. Then thematically, one subject after another. And then demographically, one personality after another. She begins to see the story of radical feminism at Priestly—what happened, who did it, and why. Though the story appears to emerge all on its own, she has the sense that she is in fact constructing it. Her mother, a member of the Women's Liberation Army, experienced the past she is studying. She, together with myriad other people, places, and things, was there. But Elizabeth was not. All she experiences is the artifacts of the past, the things that by design and chance have survived into her present. These include her own mother and her mother's memories about that past. Most of these artifacts are not, however, people and their memories. They are things: newspapers, pamphlets, posters, reports, memos, photos, letters—in a word, documents.

This realization prompts two further reflections. First, she begins to understand that many—indeed most—of the relevant artifacts have not been passed down to her present. She finds numerous references in the documents to other papers that she is unable to find and is more or less certain no longer exist. Most of the past, it turns out, has vanished without a trace. That, she thinks, is a sobering thought for anyone trying to write a story about the past and should be borne in mind by anyone reading such a story. Second, she realizes that the few artifacts that have survived have been utterly stripped of the context that produced them. They are like orphans who cannot tell you who their parents were, where they lived, or what they did. The documents are in this sense mute, and the only way you can understand them is to try to relate them to things they brought with them into the present, that is, to other surviving documents. Out of these few and tenuous relations, Elizabeth has to build a world anew.

And then, finally, she is reminded of something she learned in a seminar at Hornblower, namely, that there is an important difference between the past and a story about the past. The past is complete in itself. It contains everything that happened, an unimaginably large and complex set of things and relationships between things that moved through a specific time. The past is also, however, physically inaccessible. You can't go there and look around; the historian is always stuck in the present. It follows that all you can know about the past must be in the present. And here's the rub from Elizabeth's and every historian's point of view: almost all of the past vanished as it made its way to the present, and what little survived has been ripped out of its original context. It is impossible, then, to "reconstruct" the past. All that the historian can do is tell a story about a tiny part of the past, namely, that part which survives in the present. All histories, Elizabeth thinks, are stories about the past; but no history is the whole story about the past, for such a thing cannot exist.

All this heady philosophizing weighs heavily on Elizabeth's mind. She's not so much worried about the fact that the evidence is partial and without context; this is true in many disciplines, even in the hard sciences. Nobody's "data set" is really complete. It's the business about having to tell a story that gives her the willies. Not only are there a lot of different kinds of stories—happy ones, sad ones, triumphal ones, tragic ones—but there seem to be a lot of different stories in the material she's investigating. There's the story about the birth, life, and death of the radical feminist groups themselves. There's the story about popular and official reactions to the groups. There's the story about the political infighting in the groups. There's the story about government efforts to spy on and even undermine the groups. There's the story about the evolution of party line among group intellectuals and leaders. There's the story about how the groups raised funds. There's the story of group publications. There's the story of the groups' relationships with other groups. And of course there are all the stories of the people involved: how they became interested in radical feminism, what they did "at the Revolution," whom they loved and hated, what became of them when it was all over.

The documents in the archive tell Elizabeth which stories she *can* tell, but they don't give her much guidance on which story she *should* tell. To answer this question, Elizabeth fell back on something her advisor said to her once: a historian should uncover and teach stories about the past that are relevant to present concerns *sine ira et studio*. Except for the Latin part (which, Elizabeth later learned, means "without anger or bias"), these instructions seemed reasonably clear: find a topic that matters and then report on it neutrally. Upon reflection, however, Elizabeth realized that they weren't clear at all.

What matters? Unlike some hard scientific disciplines, history has no well-defined set of problems that matter to the field in whole or in large part. The Clay Mathematics Institute asked a bunch of experts what the most important math problems were. They identified seven; if you solve one, Clay will give you a million dollars. Nothing similar exists for history. If you asked a bunch of historians what the most important unsolved questions in history are, they'd look at you like you were crazy. It's true that history has some classic questions, for example, "Why did the Roman Empire fall?" or "What were the causes of the French Revolution?" No historian, however, can answer these questions to the satisfaction of all other historians. What matters in history seems to really depend on whom you ask. Ask a Russian and they are likely to say Russian history. Ask an African American and they are likely to say African-American history. Ask a gay activist and they are likely to say queer history. As a rule, people are interested in the history of their people, whoever their people might be. So to ask, "What history matters to you?" is to a large degree the same as asking, "Who are you?"

And what is neutral? Elizabeth knows that the very act of selecting one story to tell of the many possible stories demonstrates a bias. In opting to study radical feminist groups, then, she's already been something other than neutral. Since there would seem to be nothing she can do about this other than to study nothing, she's not particularly upset about this transgression. She is a bit perplexed, however, concerning how she—an avowed feminist—is to remain neutral while she studies and writes about feminism. She knows the rules: don't make things up or willfully distort the record; don't make political statements or render judgments implicitly based on political values; don't use coded language to imply that certain historical actors were villains or heroes. But Elizabeth wonders if following these rules will really enable her to produce a neutral history. She believes that following them will give her book the appearance of neutrality but not neutrality itself. She's a feminist. That's one of the main reasons she studies women's history, selected radical feminism as her dissertation topic, and hopes to write and publish a history book based on it. She's got a dog in the fight and she's uncomfortable pretending she doesn't. Apparently, however, that's what's required, so that's what she'll do.

After about a year in the archives, she has everything she believes she needs to write her dissertation. In any case, she's out of money. So she says goodbye to her Priestly friends and heads back to Hornblower. She's now a "G6," meaning her funding will run out in a year. She applies for and receives a Pittlebutt Dissertation Write-Up Grant and begins teaching sections of "American Civilization II." That should keep the lights on for another two or more years. She's got a good sketch of each chapter of the dissertation. She begins writing.

It's lonely, grinding work. Her plan was to write every day for five hours, but she finds that the most she can put in is about three. She leaves her little studio apartment to teach, make forays to the library, and attend the occasional department seminar. She watches a lot of TV and begins to have a glass or two of wine every night. She has no social life, and this begins to worry her. She's 28 years old and, as her mother reminds her gently, her "biological clock" is ticking. She's had boyfriends, but has never found the right guy. And now with the dissertation eating her life, she has no time—not to mention energy—to search for the right guy. She looks around her and sees that many of the female professors at Hornblower are single and have no children. She respects their decisions (if they were decisions), but she doesn't want to end up that way. She joins a dating site but goes on no dates. She begins to read blogs on the work-life balance for career women. They make her feel anxious. She fights this anxiety by pouring herself into her work, work her advisor assures her is very important. She hopes it's important enough to merit all the sacrifices she seems to be making. Feeling depressed, she decides to go to a psychiatrist, not so much for counseling as to get a script for an antidepressant a friend of hers told her about. The psychiatrist listens carefully to her story and decides that, indeed, she suffers from depression. The script is written, the pharmacy visited, the pills are taken. They help. And though the bottle clearly says, "Not to be taken with alcohol," she figures it couldn't hurt to continue her nightly libation.

Elizabeth writes draft-chapter after draft-chapter, submitting one after another to Professor Barfield over a period of many months. Her advisor is pleased with her progress, though she takes her time in getting the chapters back with suggestions for revisions. She's very busy. When they come back, though, they are full of useful commentary. Elizabeth incorporates some of her advisor's suggestions and ignores others. She's glad Professor Barfield insists that each chapter only go through one round of revision before the final reading of the entire manuscript; that really speeds things along. As the chapters accumulate, Elizabeth finds she needs to harmonize them, making sure that she doesn't repeat material in one chapter that appears in another. This is a real problem because she can't remember what she's written from one chapter to the next. And then there is all the technical, nit-picky stuff. The citations all must be checked and double checked. They must be made bibliographically complete and uniform. The title page, table of contents, chapter headers, subchapter headers, block quotes, font-styles, font-sizes, page margins, images, figures, footnote formats, and bibliography all need to be brought into conformity with the ridiculous university guidelines for dissertations. As expert as she has become in the use of word-processing programs, it still takes her an entire frustrating day to get the pagination right on the entire thing. She had four glasses of wine that night.

And at last it happens. A full nine years after she arrived at Hornblower, Elizabeth completes her dissertation: *From Young Ladies to Wild Womyn: Radical Feminism on American College Campuses, 1961 to 1975*. It's 456 double-spaced pages long, has 383 footnotes, and includes 304 items in its bibliography. With an uncharacteristic spring in her step, she marches into her advisor's office and hands it over. It's quite a moment. Professor Barfield says, "Congratulations, Elizabeth. I'll read it over and get back to you soon. I doubt there will be any major revisions because I've already read it."

Her dissertation defense follows a month later. She's been told that it's nothing but a formality. Indeed that's what it turns out to be. She and her committee sit around a banged-up table in the department's seminar room. She dresses up for the occasion, though no one else has bothered. There's some polite banter, a few earnest questions, and it's over. She's asked to leave the room. A few minutes elapse and she's called back to a chorus of congratulations. Every one shakes her hand. One of the professors makes a point of calling her "Dr. Ranke." Elizabeth detects a note of irony in his voice, though perhaps she's being paranoid. Everyone parts company. Elizabeth goes out that night with her friends to celebrate. She gets really drunk and sings karaoke until she's hoarse. She doesn't remember coming home, though she wakes up in her apartment. On the first day of the rest of her life, she's alone and hungover. But she has done what she set out to do—she's written a history book.

Chapter 4

Making a Living as a History-Book Writer

Finding someone to pay you to be a historian is like playing Russian roulette, only you don't die if you lose. You just continue on miserably.
—Reinhardt Friedrich Freiherr von Teufel

Elizabeth Ranke, now PhD, must find a way to put bread on the table writing history books. She knows the hard truth: most people who are trained to write history books never make a living as history-book writers. For many years now the number of new history PhDs has far exceeded the number of jobs available to them. The "job crisis" in history is not a "crisis" at all. It's a chronic disease. Elizabeth knows this and it scares her. She wants to be a professor, full stop. She did not labor in the trenches of graduate school for almost a decade to work at an insurance company. She feels she deserves a job in a history department, and so does her advisor. Her work is "terrific." She has no Plan B anymore; she feels she's too old for law school. Elizabeth is, as gamblers say, "all in."

When applying to graduate school, Elizabeth wisely sought counsel and aid from her undergraduate mentor. Said counsel and aid proved very useful. So, when "going out" on the job market, Elizabeth again seeks council and aid, this time from her graduate advisor. This, as it happens, proves less effective. All Professor Barfield could say was that Elizabeth should apply for every relevant job opening announced in the Historical Society of the United State's (HSUS) newsletter, *Viewpoint*. Big schools and small schools, prestigious schools and third-tier schools, well-located schools and schools in the boonies—apply to them all indiscriminately if they advertised a job even close to her field.

Naturally Professor Barfield would do what she could to improve Elizabeth's chances: write her a good recommendation, advise her on what to put in her letter of application and CV, and give her tips on interviewing. But, she suggested, most of this wouldn't matter much, particularly in the early, crucial stages of the job-getting process. All the candidates would have good recommendations, excellent cover letters and CVs, and know how to impress in interviews.

"What does really matter?" Elizabeth asked. And here, for the first time ever, Elizabeth saw Professor Barfield speak with a note of cynicism. History hiring committees often receive hundreds of applications for one position. There is no question of reading all the applications; there just isn't enough time. Besides, it's not really necessary. What is necessary, at least early in the selection process, is to look at three key signals in the applications.

The first of these signals is where the applicant went to graduate school. The meaning of this signal varies according to the rank of the school doing the selection. Prestigious schools and schools that aspire to be prestigious are very concerned with maintaining (in the former case) or building (in the latter case) an elite brand. Such a brand enables them to attract the best students, who then become the most successful people, who then donate the most money to their *almae matres*. For this reason they strongly prefer candidates from peer institutions or from their supposed betters. Candidates from these schools are not going to run off in search of better jobs, for, practically speaking, there are no better jobs to be had. In contrast, obscure schools are quite concerned with faculty retention. They know that status really matters in academia and that they have little status to offer. So they prefer candidates from respectable though not elite graduate programs. These candidates are not going to run off in search of better jobs because they know they will almost never get them, not having attended elite graduate programs.

The second signal, Professor Barfield says, is the title of the dissertation. Not the topic, she stresses, but the title itself. This little piece of information is very useful in "cutting" the pile of applications in a number of ways. To begin with, it allows committee members to throw out applicants who did not read the job description as it was intended to be read. Now this, Professor Barfield says, is tricky. In the easiest cases, the dissertation title suggests that the candidate obviously doesn't "do" the main field advertised: no one is going to hire an early American historian for a modern American history position. Most cases, however, are more difficult. Faculties often can't agree on what they want from a candidate: the American diplomatic historian wants a diplomatic historian; the American women's historian wants a women's historian; the American labor historian wants a labor historian and so on. For this reason, job descriptions often contain a confused, seemingly accidental jumble of fields in addition to the main one on offer. The title of the dissertation will tell a committee member whether a particular candidate does one of the subfields in the description; if they don't, then they get thrown out of the pile. The title will also tell a committee member whether the candidate does one of their pet subjects. The American diplomatic historian wants an American diplomatic historian, but she really wants someone who does American relations with Asia, because that's what she does. Two scholars working in this subfield could, she will argue, give the department a strength that can be leveraged in graduate admissions and national ranking. Again, the title tells her what she needs to know.

The final signal is the candidate's gender and race. HSUS prints its official policy strictly forbidding discrimination on the basis of gender and race in every issue of *Viewpoint*, appropriately enough right before the job listings. Nonetheless, many job descriptions contain language such as: "Women and minorities are encouraged to apply." This sort of thing is allowed because HSUS also has a policy permitting schools to pursue "institutional goals" promoting fair representation of women and minorities, in other words, affirmative action in hiring. It's likely that virtually all the members of a hiring committee and department agree that affirmative action is a good thing. But what they think doesn't really matter much, because every university's Equal Opportunity and Diversity Office will check to make sure that everything is fair and square and that "institutional goals" are met.

The EODO monitors every search a department conducts. It will require the search committee to present two lists during the hiring process: the long list of all applicants and the short list of candidates to be interviewed on campus. If women or minorities are not to be found in the right proportions on these lists, the EODO will raise a red flag. The committee knows this and would just as soon avoid the hassle of explaining why it did what it did. So it makes sure that the lists contain everyone the EODO thinks it should in the right measure. Interestingly, the EODO's preference for female and minority candidates can work in the department's favor. Imagine that the department, upon interviewing three candidates on campus, ranks a white male first, a black female second, and a white male third. The department could offer the job to the first-ranked white male and then go to EODO to request that the second-ranked black female be offered a job as an "opportunity hire." If the administration agrees, the department has gotten two "lines" (as full-time faculty jobs are called) where it was offered only one.

Elizabeth, feeling increasingly uncomfortable, interrupts her advisor. "It seems to me," she says, "that this entire process is not only unfair, it's also hypocritical and arbitrary." Professor Barfield smiles knowingly and responds, "Yes, you're right. But we've got pick candidates somehow. Besides, you're not in bad shape at all." Elizabeth went to an esteemed graduate program, so she's already in the door at first- and second-tier departments with job openings in her field. Moreover, Elizabeth's dissertation title says all the right things: it identifies her plainly as a modern American women's historian, and that's a hot and growing field. Finally, Elizabeth is a woman. That doesn't help as much as it used to because history departments are now nearly all gender balanced. But the professoriate at large is not, so women are still given special preference in the dean's office.

"As for arbitrary," Professor Barfield says, "I'm not done yet." Once the candidate list has been cut from, say, 200 applicants to 30 or so, the hard work begins. The committee starts to look at all the submitted material in detail. They analyze the candidates' CVs, their cover letters, their writing samples, and their letters of recommendation. These materials give the committee members something relatively substantive to talk about when it comes to ranking candidates. Some applicants, for example, will have won nationally recognized fellowships or even post-docs and some will not; some will clearly outline how they are going to turn their dissertations into books and others will not; some are going to sketch promising "second projects" and others will not; some will "be able to write" and others will not; and some will have great letters from stars in their fields and others will not. "This process," Professor Barfield assures Elizabeth, "is only somewhat arbitrary, and certainly less arbitrary than the first cut." The history profession has generally recognized standards, and the committee has now gotten down to applying them rigorously. Of course it should apply them rigorously to all applicants. But that, alas, is just not possible. There are too many of them.

At the end of this stage in the hiring process, the committee will arrive at an interview list of around a dozen candidates. The interviews take place at one or another annual convention, often HSUS's big meeting. These confabs are primarily intended to offer scholars a place to present research papers to their colleagues in innumerable, topic-specific sessions. They are also forums to meet, greet, and exchange gossip. For most attendees, they are a lot of fun; for job candidates, they are anything but. Job seekers are understandably nervous. You can often see them milling about in their uncomfortable interview suits, anxiously awaiting their fateful appointments. They talk to one another, trying to maintain a brave face. The chief subject of conversation, of course, is who got what interview where. Candidates with several interviews are glad to tell you so; candidates who made the long, expensive trip for one interview are more reticent. Everyone is freaked out.

If they are lucky, the candidates will be interviewed in the calm of an unimaginably appointed suite in the convention hotel. If not, the interview will take place in the meeting center, a large, loud, drab hall subdivided into many little booths, each one occupied by a search committee. In this case the candidates make themselves known at the registry desk shortly before the appointed time and wait to be called by one of the attendants. It's very awkward, for they really have nothing to do with themselves but stew. And they may have to stew for quite a while. Once a group of historians gets to talking, it's hard to get them to stop. So it is that the interviews—which are supposed to last between fifteen and thirty minutes—routinely run over, thereby completely disrupting the schedule. It could be worse, however, and sometimes it is. Some schools are either too poor or too organizationally incompetent to reserve a booth in the cattle-call room. They tell candidates to meet them in the hotel lobby, café, or even bar. This sort of thing is strictly forbidden by the HSUS, but, alas, the HSUS never seems to be watching.

The interviews themselves are anodyne, rushed affairs. They begin with introductions, greetings, and apologies. "Hi, I'm Greg Scotchbright. So glad to meet you. Sorry for the delay, but we're running a bit late." Further apologies may be necessary if one of the interviewers is absent, not an unusual occurrence. "Professor Bittlebaum had to step out, he'll be back shortly." Usually the candidate never sees Professor Bittlebaum. Then to business. The committee head ensures the candidate that everyone has carefully considered everything submitted. "We read all your stuff and it's terrific." They then ask the candidate to talk about his or her work as if they have no idea what it is about. A prepared oration ensues in which the candidate summarizes his or her 400-page dissertation in three minutes or so and assures the committee that he or she is preparing the manuscript for publication. Generally, the committee asks no questions about that work because they haven't read it or, if they have, don't remember it. All agree, however, that it sounds "fascinating." Then there are some perfunctory questions. "Tell us about what you would like to teach." "Can you talk about your next project?" And the ever popular: "Why do you want to teach at our university?" The candidate is naturally ready to answer all these questions, though in doing so finds that he can barely be heard over the din of other interviewees answering the exact same questions in the adjoining booths. Then the head of the search suddenly interjects, "Oh my God, we're already over time," and the interview is over. Everyone says, "Nice to meet you," and the head adds, "We'll be in touch."

"It doesn't sound like you learn very much during these interviews," Elizabeth remarks. "Well," Professor Barfield replies, "you do and you don't." The convention interviews, she explains, are not really meant to judge a candidate's potential as a scholar or teacher, but rather to give an impression of what kind of colleague he or she might be. On the most superficial level, the committee is simply asking, "Does this person know the basics of academic decorum?" If they are poorly dressed, don't shake hands, and constantly interrupt, those are all bad signs. On a deeper level, the committee is asking, "Is this person smart enough to be in our department?" Here the way the candidates speak is all important, as most historians equate eloquence with intelligence. If the applicant fumbles over words, that's bad; if he or she speaks in well-formed paragraphs, that's good. "And there is one other thing the interviews are useful for," Professor

Barfield says with some hesitation, "but you didn't hear it from me." It's often the case that committee members can't tell whether a candidate is a minority or not from his or her application. Seeing them in the flesh tells them exactly what they need to know.

"What happens then?" Elizabeth asks. The committee deliberates, trades horses, and makes a ranked short list of three or four candidates to bring to campus. "Then," Professor Barfield says, "you get the call or you don't. If you don't, you try to figure out what you're going to do next. If you do, then you've got to prepare for your fly-out." Since the committee will almost certainly ask for a candidate's dissertation at this stage, that must be promptly sent. Then there's some detective work to be done. The applicant needs to find out all he or she can about the search committee members, particularly what they work on. This will give the candidate something to talk about with the committee members and will demonstrate that he or she has "done her homework." Finally, the applicant needs to decide on, draft, and practice his or her "talk." The talk—a formal lecture often given before the entire department—is crucial. Only the search committee will read the candidate's dissertation. The rest of the department will merely hear the talk. The committee will probably make its recommendation to the department largely on the basis of the dissertation, research being the most important factor at this stage in the game, especially at an elite school. The department, however, will approve or reject that recommendation on the basis of the talk, which is all it knows about the candidate's research. Since the dissertation is done and in the hands of the committee, there is nothing an applicant can do on that score. But the talk provides a fresh opportunity to win points with the department.

The fly-out itself is a highly scripted affair in which the script is occasionally disregarded by the actors. On the day of arrival, there will be a dinner with several faculty members at a local restaurant. This event is essentially an opportunity for the candidate to make a mistake. "So don't talk too much," Professor Barfield advises. The department members, of course, cannot make a mistake because they know that you'll take the job if they offer it. This can lead to some bad behavior, especially if one or more of them have a few drinks. Professor Barfield then recalls how at one such dinner a colleague told a joke about Lyndon Johnson's penis. After dinner, off to bed, though probably not right to sleep. The next day is full of meetings: with members of the department, some graduate students, a librarian or two, and a dean. Only the meetings with the faculty members and grad students make any difference. Again, they are opportunities to make a mistake, so it's best not to say too much and to be very friendly. If the school has no graduate program, the department may ask a candidate to teach an undergraduate class, a bewildering experience because the undergraduates have no idea why someone other than their regular teacher is talking to them. Finally, there's the "talk" itself, which is, of course, another opportunity to make a mistake. Professor Barfield kindly offers a list of things not to do in a talk: don't read your paper, rather appear to speak extemporaneously; don't use a computer, because computers cause mishaps; don't argue with anyone about anything, rather concede a "good question" and say, "I'll need to look into that." After the talk, it's off to the final dinner. "You may want to have a glass of wine," says Professor Barfield, "but just one. You don't want to find yourself uncontrollably telling a joke about Lyndon Johnson's member." The next morning the candidate wings it home.

"And then?" Elizabeth asks. The committee deliberates. Since they already had a ranking before the "fly-outs," the question is whether anything learned during the "fly-outs" should move them to alter that ranking. Usually they stand pat unless someone in the top two spots made a number of missteps. Then the committee presents its decision to the full department in a grand meeting. One after another, the faculty members weigh in. Some of them will talk about how impressed they were with one of the candidates' research, how wonderful their "talk" was, or how well they answered questions. But most of the comments boil down to, "I liked her more than the other two, so we should offer her the job." A sense of personal connection matters a lot at this stage in the process. So does a feeling that the candidate will "fit in." After everyone has had their say, the department chair will either announce that consensus has been reached or he will call a vote. If the vote is close, then they may keep talking until a clear majority emerges.

"So," Elizabeth says, "I've got to make them like me? But what if I've already published a book? What if I've taught a lot? What if I've done excellent committee work?" Professor Barfield sighs. "None of that will matter if they don't like you, and it could, oddly enough, hurt you." In most lines of work, experience counts for a lot, as it's a pretty good indicator that an applicant can do the job. The person with more and better experience often gets the nod. But not in history. Committees routinely throw very experienced candidates out of the pile during the first or second cut. Why is this? The answer is that seasoned candidates have records, and records can be criticized. The committee knows where they stand, and if they don't like where they stand, then out they go. The fact that other scholars—those who reviewed their articles, vetted their books, recommended them for promotion—think they are terrific is irrelevant; what the committee thinks is all that bears any weight. In contrast, freshly minted PhDs with nothing but dissertations have no records. They are still unknown quantities, pure "potential." Committees love candidates with "great potential" because they can imagine those candidates realizing that potential in their own depart-ments. "Of course," Professor Barfield confesses, "applicants with 'great potential' often turn out to be mediocre scholars and poor colleagues. But you know what they say, 'Hope springs eternal.'"

"Okay," Elizabeth says, "I'm pretty likeable and completely inexperienced, so I'm in good shape. What happens after the fly-out?" "After checking with EODO one last time, the department makes an offer," Professor Barfield says. "If you get a phone call, that's probably good news; if you get an e-mail, that's probably bad news." In the former case, the department will send the applicant an offer letter and give her between a week and month to negotiate and decide. A shorter period indicates that the department has a very promising candidate waiting in second place; a longer period indicates the department really wants the candidate in the first place. Usually, however, they get their first choice for a very simple reason: most job candidates get no offers, and those that do usually only get one. If offered a job, then, they will take it and be grateful. Since "this or nothing" is not a very strong negotiating position, a candidate doesn't have a lot of leverage in negotiations. She might get a tiny salary bump, a fatter start-up package, or a shorter tenure clock. Then again they may get "take it or leave it," in which case they will take it. "No matter where it is?" Elizabeth asks. "No matter where it is," her advisor confirms.

Elizabeth asks another question: "But what if the new hire is married or in a relationship? Does the university help her partner find a job nearby?" Professor Barfield looks pensively out the window onto the quad. "No, not usually. Academia is sort of a home-wrecker." She goes on to explain how she had a partner when she first arrived at Hornblower from Westcostia. Her partner did not want to move: she had a good job as a museum curator, and good jobs as museum curators are hard to find. Barfield asked a dean to help, and the dean said he would. Nothing came of it, though. Barfield's partner applied for many positions in museums at Hornblower and in the surrounding area. Nothing came of that, either. They tried to commute back and forth, but the travel was both too expensive and too hard. In the end they broke up. "I never thought I'd say it, but I'm glad I don't have a boyfriend," Elizabeth said.

"So once you're hired, it's all clover, right?" Though Elizabeth meant this question as a joke, Professor Barfield doesn't laugh. She simply says, "Not exactly, but the hard part is over, you've beaten the odds, and things get a lot easier." This surprises Elizabeth. "But what about all the teaching, committee work, publishing your book, and getting tenure?" she asks. "Nothing to really worry about," her advisor responds.

As for teaching, most new hires already know how to do it because they've either done it in graduate school or at other institutions. They just need to do what they did before and not make any obvious blunders. Besides, teaching matters little in tenure cases except at elite liberal arts colleges. As for committee work, departments routinely do not assign it, or at least much of it, to pre-tenure faculty. They do this because they want their hires to get tenure and thereby show the deans that they are picking their faculty well. As for publishing a book, this is not difficult. Good dissertations do not need much reworking to become publishable manuscripts; and almost any publishable manuscript can find a publisher. True, revision will take some time, and the reviser might not get his or her first, second, or even third choice of publishers. But probationary faculty have a lot of time and there are a lot of publishers out there. And as for getting tenure, almost everybody does if they have a book under contract or already out. Of course the university tenure guidelines say that teaching, service, and research are to be weighted equally in tenure cases, but no one pays much attention to that. Teaching is hard to assess beyond "Did enough of it and the students didn't all hate her." Service is not a factor because, as we've seen, probationary faculty don't do much of it. And that leaves research, which, for all intents and purposes, means writing and publishing books. Outside very picky, very prestigious, and very elite research universities, a single monograph published by almost any university press is the universal standard for the granting of tenure. And if a historian happens to be at one of those very picky, very prestigious, very elite research universities and fails to get tenure (not at all an unusual occurrence), then he or she can be pretty sure that they can trade the status of having been at a first-tier school to get a tenured job in a second-tier school.

"That's very comforting," Elizabeth says, "but what happens if I don't get a job?" Calling on her knowledge of Marxism and natural wit, Professor Barfield quips, "You join the labor army of unemployed historians, temporarily we hope." Since most recent history PhDs don't get tenure-track jobs, their numbers build up year after year creating a vast pool of under-used historical talent. There is great sympathy among tenured history faculty for these unfortunate people; not enough for them to cut the number of new graduate students they accept, but sympathy nonetheless. They will, therefore, do three things to help PhDs at loose ends. First, they will try to drum up work for them in their home departments, for example teaching sections in large lecture classes or, exceptionally, teaching an actual course. The difficulty here is that every section given to an unemployed PhD is a section that can't be given to a newly arrived graduate student — there's only so much work to go around. Second, sympathetic advisors will encourage their unemployed students to apply for adjunct jobs. University administrators are under constant pressure to keep costs low and the number of students enrolled high. The existence of a labor army of unemployed PhDs desperate to continue their careers allows them to do both. Instead of funding expensive new lines, they give departments money to hire remarkably inexpensive adjuncts. Of course the departments would rather have the lines, but they are powerless. Finally, faculty members will tell their footloose PhDs to seek out what are essentially post-docs called by the name "fellowships." The number and competitiveness of these depend on the field in question: popular fields like American history will have a bunch of them, but they will be hard to get; obscure fields like Inner Asian history will have many fewer and they will not be terribly competitive.

"Generally speaking," professor Barfield continues, "these three sources are sufficient to keep a large minority of unemployed PhDs in the game for one, two, or even multiple years." The majority leak out of the pipeline and run off to God-knows-where. It's hard to say who is lucky here, those who manage to stay or those who leak out. After all, the stayers may have to move several times, put their personal lives on hold, and live in relative poverty, but then again they are probably used to that after, say, ten years in graduate school. "In addition to the hardship," Professor Barfield warns, "there are additional dangers to holding on in this way." Every time a candidate goes out on the job market and doesn't get a job, he is being visibly passed over. Needless to say this may have nothing to do with the quality of the candidate; it could, given the nature of the hiring process, just be bad luck. Nonetheless, the more times a job seeker is passed over, the less desirable they will appear to status-conscious search committees. Nothing succeeds like success, and nothing fails like failure. Just as disturbingly, the obvious strategy to improve one's credentials—namely, publishing a lot—could easily backfire. A well-published applicant who has been on the job market for a few years no longer has any "potential." Rather, they have established and growing records—records that can be scrutinized by search committees looking for likes and dislikes. A book will get a tenure-track historian tenure; a book will not, probably, get someone who has been passed over several times a tenure-track job.

"All of this sounds truly awful," Elizabeth remarks. "What about being a historian and writing history books outside the academy?" Professor Barfield sighs. "A historian outside the academy is like a barber without a barbershop." There are historians who manage to make a living writing history books. There are not very many of them, though, and it's not hard to see why. Writing serious books in general is a hard way to pay the bills. If someone says to you, "I'm a writer," you can be pretty sure that, unless he lives on a park bench, he has some source of income other than writing serious books. Most people who have the intelligence and drive to write a good book have the intelligence and drive to do something else, something that pays, so that's what they end up doing. As concerns history books, they often sell pretty well; readers like history. But they like some kinds of history a lot more than others. That means the would-be popular historian who does not want to live on a park bench has to write to the people's tastes. What do people want in history books: biographies of famous people, stuff about wars and battles, stories about well-known tragedies and disasters, and, perhaps, a bit of politics, preferably slanted hard to the Right or Left.

Interestingly, these are topics that historians-in-training are told to avoid and about which, once they becomes professional historians, they almost never write. Academic historians view themselves as elite professionals. They write for the ages, not for the people. They will not pander, and they will look down their noses at those they think are pandering. In the eyes of many academic historians, the panderers-in-chief are the so-called popular historians. These folks come in two varieties. First there are the "amateurs": people who write history, so to say, without a license (a PhD, that is). They write sub-par history but can be excused because they don't know how to do any better. Second there are the "sellouts" — people who, though they hold the PhD, write history for the masses. By the lights of academic historians, they are the worst of the worst, particularly if their books are very widely read and commonly reviewed in national magazines and newspapers. Academic historians will give lip service to the "significant contribution" so-and-so makes by writing popular history, but behind these words there is often contempt, condescension, and jealousy. Truman Capote is said to have quipped:

"Whenever one of my friends succeeds, I die a little bit inside." So it is with many academic historians.

"So if I try to write history books that sell I'll probably fail, and if I don't, I'll get dissed?" Elizabeth asks. "Exactly so," Professor Barfield responds, "though 'dissed' is not a word I would get into the habit of using." "Okay. So what else is there for a history PhD who wants to ply her trade?" Elizabeth queries. "Not much," her advisor admits. Though HSUS is always going on about "history careers outside the academy," there really aren't many of them that truly involve historical work. There are museums. They sometimes have historians on-staff, but often they don't if they do not deal in matters historical. There are archives. One can find history PhDs working in them, though much more frequently one finds people with degrees in library science. There is the military. All the branches employ historians, though they all do military history. Finally, there is the government, or rather some of the agencies thereof. A few of them, such as the State Department, have historians to chronicle their business; most don't.

Elizabeth says nothing and neither does Professor Barfield. There's nothing much to say because it is now clear what Elizabeth must do: apply for every available academic job remotely related to her work and hope she gets lucky. Her chances are about one in two, probably as good as they will ever be. If she doesn't land a position this year, she can apply next. The odds that she can get some teaching, an adjunct position, or a fellowship to hold her over are quite good. But every year she goes out on the job market and fails to bring home the tenure-track prize, her chances of ever doing so will likely diminish. She will go from a scholar full of "promise" to a candidate who, for whatever accidental reason, has been passed over. She could try to publish her way out of this vexing situation. That, she knows, is a dangerous strategy, for it only provides material for her potential critics on search committees. As the years mount, the pressure to leave the field will grow. But where will she go? She doesn't want to work in a museum even if she could get a job in one. She wants to write history books and earn a good living doing it, and here there is really only one good option: get a tenure-track job in a history department.

As it happened, Elizabeth did. Not her first year out, sorry to say. That year she got a fellowship from a well-known American Studies center at an equally well-known university. But the next season her number came up. She submitted 32 applications and got one offer—that, she consoled herself, is all you need. It was a middle-tier state school in one of those Midwestern states that begins with the letter "i." Its veterinary school is ranked among the top in the nation. Elizabeth found the small city in which it was located strange. She'd never seen a tractor driving in a town. And on certain fall weekends the streets teemed with drunken, stumbling football fans. The natives, however, were friendly, you could get a good cup of coffee, and they sold organic groceries at the local food co-op. She worked hard teaching, sitting on committees, and turning her dissertation into a publishable book. She got tenure even though she only had a book contract, not the book itself. But the book was eventually published. She had reached her life's goal: she was a professional history-book writer.

Chapter 5

The Parts of a History Book

The only part of a history book most people read is the introduction.
If it's a good book, that's all they'll need to read.
—Reinhardt Friedrich Freiherr von Teufel

Elizabeth Ranke, now an associate professor, has succeeded in writing and publishing a history book. Her book is different from all others: she is, in fact, the only historian to have ever written at length on radical feminism at Priestly in the 1960s. Yet in other ways her book is exactly the same as countless others, most notably in that it has the same parts. Modern history books are written and published according to a template, and each element of that template has a particular function. What are, then, the parts of a modern history book and what do they mean?

Let's begin with the cover. Despite what you might have heard, you can in fact judge about a book by its cover. If, on the one hand, the cover is hard and has no jacket that probably means the editor thinks only libraries will buy it. The editor knows that librarians immediately discard book jackets on the well-grounded logic that patrons will sooner-or-later (and probably sooner) do the same. Thus, they figure, there is no point in going to the expense of designing and printing a fancy jacket. And the nakedness of the cover is not the only element that suggests the editor's target market is the librarian crowd. There is also the fact that the book costs $160. Only a librarian, and a well-funded one, could conceivably bear that burden.

If, on the other hand, the book has a soft cover, that likely signals that the editor thinks the public, or rather a small portion thereof, might buy it. The editor knows that, although history buffs will recoil at a $160 jacketless book on a compelling subject, they might just pick up a $25 paperback on the same compelling subject if presented with an equally compelling cover. In fact, the books might be one and the same, content-wise, just marketed in two ways. This "different-format-for-different-markets" strategy is standard operating procedure in the book industry.

If, on the third hand (so to say), the book is hardback and jacketed, that means the editor wants to have it both ways. She thinks she can get both libraries and history buffs to buy it in profitable numbers if she markets it at just the right price—say, $35—and with the right promotional material—that is, a fancy jacket. Make no mistake about it, book jackets are advertise-ments. They are meant to catch the eye of book browsers by using arresting graphics, bold fonts, and flashy (though not garish) colors. The jacket designer's hope is that, your attention being drawn, you will pick the book up for further investigation. If you do, you'll find other advertising devices meant to get you to carry it to the register and buy it.

On the front of the jacket, of course, you will find the author's name and the book's title. The latter, if you know how to decode it, will tell you a lot. You almost never see a history book with a title plain and simple, that is, an unbroken series of words like *The History of the Decline and Fall of the Roman Empire*. If that's what you have, then what you have is either old (as with Gibbon's work) or new and trying desperately to draw attention to itself by being knowingly unfashionable. Since the editors who make book titles are herd animals, they don't generally like to appear unfashionable.

The almost universal formula for naming history books today is this: *[Short Title]: [Subtitle]*. The short title must be, well, short: *Westcostia at War*, *A Time to Die*, *Reckless Empire*, *To Win the Race*, and so on. Elizabeth's short title—*From Young Ladies to Wild Womyn*—is a bit on the long side, but it will due. If the short title gives you a fair idea of what the book is about (as in the case of

Westcostia at War), then it's probably written by a popular historian and published by a trade press. These folks make their livings selling books, so they hew to punchy, telegraphic short titles. If the short title alone gives you little idea regarding the book's subject (as with *A Time to Die*), then it's probably written by an academic and published by a university press. Professors and university press editors are under very little pressure to sell books to the public, so they have near free rein to craft the short titles as they will. They place a premium on being dramatic and clever. *A Time to Die* and *Reckless Empire* are both dramatic and therefore good short titles. Only *To Win the Race* is dramatic and clever, though, for it is a book about African-American politicians. For those who can't find the right dramatic and clever short title, there is now a ready formula that will work for almost anything: *X Matters*, where X is some subject. So we have *Race Matters, Class Matters, Gender Matters, Socks Matter, Shoes Matter, Laces Matter*, etc. One wonders how far this can go, for pretty soon every matter will matter and therefore nothing will truly matter any more than any other matter. Not that it matters, because almost no one reads these books.

The subtitle of a history book almost always tells you what the book is really about. That's what Elizabeth's does. It reads *Radical Feminism on American College Campuses, 1961 to 1975* and her book is, in fact, about radical feminism on American College Campuses, 1961 to 1975, sort of (see below). Popular historians and their trade press editors prefer long subtitles full of breathless excitement about what is promised inside, for they are supposed to help sell books. The subtitle of *A Time to Die* is, for example, *The Remarkable Story of the Daring Attempt to Save the Sultan of Utopistan from the Assassins of Shishkabob During the Great Conflagration of the Bygone Heroic Age*. Professional historians and their university press editors are more subdued and, on the whole, truthful about what's inside. They will, however, occasionally use the subtitle to practice a bit of deception. We can see this in the case of Elizabeth's fine book. It's not really about radical feminism on American college campuses, 1961–1975. It's really about radical feminism at the University of Westcostia, Priestly during the period. Her editor told her to widen the scope of the book without going back into the archives for a decade. And, the editor advised, the easiest way to work this magic was to state in the introduction that her book is a case study that sheds light on a much larger phenomenon. Elizabeth took said advice, though she's not sure how representative the radical feminists at Priestly actually were. Her editor tells her not to worry because, unlike all the other matters, that matter doesn't matter.

Let's move from the jacket cover to the inside front fold. There you'll encounter the "blurb." The best way to understand the blurb is to read it like a movie-trailer voice-over. Try it with this blurbish line: "Never before in the history of humankind have so few brave souls stood together against such overwhelming evil!" Sounds really dramatic, doesn't it? Historians generally hate blurbs because they intentionally simplify their "complex, nuanced, multi-threaded narratives." But that's the point; the blurb, like the title, is a hook. So don't be surprised if what you find on the inside of a history book is not exactly what was advertised in the blurb. This is, after all, advertising, and it definitely matters.

On the inside back fold, you'll often discover a picture of the author and a short biography. The former will be your standard head-and-shoulders shot. If the author is an academic, the image will probably be poorly composed and grainy. Academics feign a kind of modesty when it comes to photos of themselves. A bad photo says, "I'm not concerned with appearances; I'm all about ideas!" Since most publishers—university presses in particular—don't want to shell out the hard green to get professional photos taken of their authors, they use whatever the author supplies. Elizabeth, for example, simply sent a passport photo. She was having a bad hair day, but, being all about ideas, was unconcerned. If the author, however, is a popular historian, the photo will be of much higher quality and perhaps even professionally made. If so, then the photographer will be credited in letters almost too tiny to read. The photo may have been paid for by the author, or it may have been paid for by the trade press. In either case, the idea is that a good photo of an attractive author or one made to look attractive will help sell books and therefore is worth the investment. In truth, most historians are not much to look at, but that's another matter.

The biography immediately below the photo is meant to establish the author's bona fides or, as they say in the publicity department, her "platform." The underlying rhetoric of every author bio is this: "The author of this book is a genius who went to all the best schools, has taught and or worked at all the best places, won all the biggest honors, and has written a ton of great books, so you should really read this one." Of course most authors have not done all or perhaps any of these things. They may, however, have been fellows at the best schools, given lectures or temped at the best places, written a book or two, and won something or other. These demi-credentials are fodder for publicists, for they offer an opportunity to burnish the author's image by mere association with something of high status. Elizabeth's bio is a mixture of truth and sort-of-truth.

> Elizabeth Ranke teaches at Iowana State University. [*True*] She graduated *magna cum laude* from Twiddletwaddle College. [*True*] She took her PhD in history at Hornblower University. [*True*] She was a fellow at Oxturd University [*Sort of true*] and has lectured at St. Andrew of the Cow Patch, the Center for High Energy Metaphysics, and Funkengruven-Forschungszentrum. [*Sort of true*] She was the winner of the prestigious "Giggleheim Prize" for research in Feminist Studies. [*Sort of true*]

If the author lives in a famous hotbed of intellectual activity, this factoid will always be mentioned. Elizabeth lives in Ameless, Iowana, which is not such a place. But if she lived in Priestly, then her biography would have to end, "She lives in Priestley, Westcostia." The rhetorical *coup de grace* of this type is the ever-enviable "splits her time between place-that-means-you're-smart X and place-that-means-you're-smart Y." Though Elizabeth thinks Ameless is fine, she wouldn't mind "splitting her time" between Priestley and Oxturd. If she did, then she would write just that at the end of her bio and be proud as a peacock. Below the bio you'll often run into credits for the jacket: who designed it, where the images came from, etc. Like photographers, these folks only merit the finest of print.

On the back of the jacket the publicists continue their campaign to get you to buy the book by providing effusive endorsements—sometimes also called "blurbs"—by people they hope you've heard of. Before a book is issued, publicists send advanced copies to these people in the hopes that they will blurb the book, that is, provide some copy that can be used as an endorsement on the jacket. In the best case, famous people will write the endorsements, because everyone knows famous people know what they're talking about. Alas, publicists can rarely convince famous people to endorse history books because most famous people don't read history books. So in most cases, the publicists tap well-known popular history authors or academics who have achieved a certain standing among history buffs. How does the publicist find these people? They ask the authors. Who do the authors choose? People they know will write nice things about them. And who are those people? The authors' patrons, clients, and friends. Naturally they write things like, "This is the greatest book ever written." For example, Elizabeth's advisor blurbed her book and, not surprisingly, she thought it was a "path-breaking contribution to our understanding of post-war American history" that she "could not put down." Having friends write endorsements for each other's books may seem to invite a conflict of interest. It does. But more to the point it creates a confluence of interests of the you-scratch-my-back-I'll-scratch-yours variety. It works like this: I'll write a good blurb for your book and, when my book comes out, you can write a good blurb for mine. This kind of reciprocation is known in the trade as "log rolling," and one finds a lot of it on the back of history book jackets.

At the bottom of the jacket's back cover, you will see a number of things all having to do with the sale of the book. The first is a barcode that identifies the book for the purposes of inventory, sale, and library cataloging. Then there is the "International Standard Book Number" or "ISBN" as it's universally known. Every modern book has an ISBN. It uniquely identifies the book among the entire universe of books with ISBNs and, like the barcode, helps those who publish, sell, and catalogue books keep track of them. Finally, there is the price. Everyone knows that the price of everything changes depending on market conditions. One day your house is worth a fortune; the next day it is not. For this reason, manufacturers and retailers generally don't print prices on the items they sell; they price them according to market conditions with easily alterable things like stickers, tags, and signs. Not so publishers. They boldly print the suggested retail price of their books right below the barcode for everyone to see. Unlike every other merchant, they *know* how much their goods are worth, now and forever. Actually, they don't; they're just trying to trick you. Book publishers and sellers, like all merchants, want to make you pay as much as possible for their products. Since books are cheap to produce and distribute, they have limited options here. The one they favor is simply to proclaim authoritatively that their books are worth some figure exceeding the actual market value. This accomplishes two things. First, printing the price on the jacket suggests to gullible people that the book is actually worth whatever they say it is. Believe it or not, this ploy works some of the time. Second, printing the price on the jacket, especially a ridiculously high one, gives booksellers plenty of room to discount the book and still make a profit. Even at half the suggested price, the booksellers do pretty well.

Enough about the jacket; now let's open the book. The first couple of pages repeat what you already know—the title, the author's name—but eventually you get a new bit of information, namely, the publisher. The short name of the publisher actually appears on the book's jacket and spine. As it appears there, however, it's a bit cryptic unless you are in-the-know: what kind of press, exactly, is "Panderbilt"? On page five or so, the mystery is revealed: "Panderbilt University Press" or "Panderbilt Books." The difference is important.

If the publisher is a university press, the book is probably a monograph like Elizabeth's fine *From Young Ladies to Wild Womyn*, that is, a narrow, scholarly book, written by a scholar, and aimed at a scholarly audience. Monographs are not intended to be read, they are intended to advance the author's career within academia. Monographs are, to put it bluntly, credentials. And though monographs may not be readable or in fact ever read, they do tend to be very reliable, both because they are written by professionally-trained historians and because they have been "vetted," as they say in the peculiar jargon of academia. Vetting is a form of quality control. University press editors are not qualified to evaluate the scholarly merits of a manuscript; only experts are. For this reason, the editors send the manuscripts out to the author's peers—people who know a lot about the subject of the book—for review. To guarantee objectivity, the editors take measures to ensure the reviewers don't know who the author is and the other way around, that is, the reviews are in principle blind. The experts, usually two or three, render judgment on the book and send it to the book's editor.

This peer review process, however, is imperfect for a number of reasons. First, even before the book has been sent out for vetting, the editor has already made an evaluation. Since every would-be historian has to publish a book, editors get a lot of manuscripts. They can't publish them all, nor can they send them all out for review. So they pick and choose on the basis of criteria like the author's record, fit with the press's existing lists, and the marketability of the book. The history editor at Panderbilt UP really liked Elizabeth's book: she went to a good graduate school, her book fit the press's women's studies series well, and feminism was a pretty hot topic. She decided to send it out. What's notable here is that the editors are not, as we've indicated, peers of the author, so this isn't peer review at all. It's editorial review, which, as you might imagine, is a horse of a very different color.

But that, unfortunately, is not the worst of it. Since the editors have already shown favor on a book by deciding to send it out, they carefully select those who will evaluate it. This is what Elizabeth's would-be editor did: she selected scholars who had a reputation for writing good letters of evaluation in a timely way. There's nothing inherently wrong with this: it's certainly better to have a good reviewer than a bad one. But there is a problem if the editor chooses reviewers whom he or she thinks will like the book. Because the editors have an interest in seeing the book published — they picked it out of all other submissions — they regularly cherry pick reviews in this way. Obviously, this habit is not openly discussed. Moreover, the editors will often have a hard time making a putatively blind review actually blind in practice. History, as we've seen, is divided into numerous incestuous subfields. Everyone knows everyone else, knows what everyone else works on, and knows what everyone else's students work on. When a reviewer receives an anonymized manuscript called *The Really Big Purge* and recalls his buddy's grad student just completed a dissertation on the same topic, he puts two and two together quite easily. You might think that in such cases reviewers would recuse themselves to avoid even the appearance of bias. They don't, at least not as a matter of course.

While it is not impossible to objectively judge a dog even when you have one in a fight, it's not easy. In the present case, in fact, it's particularly difficult because the experts are not only helping decide whether the manuscript will be published, they are also deciding whether the author will get a job or be granted tenure. As we've said, nearly every would-be professional historian must publish a book to go from probationary to permanent. The evaluators know this very well, and it makes them uncomfortable. They signed up for the historical profession to write history books, not to decide people's fates. It's not hard to understand, then, that reviewers tend to go easy on the manuscripts they receive, good or bad. Ending someone's career is a heavy burden to bear, and most reviewers would rather not bear it if at all possible. And since no one is checking, it's entirely possible. In the case of *From Ladies to Wild Womyn*, the hand-picked evaluators knew Elizabeth wrote it, knew Elizabeth would be coming up for tenure soon, and knew they had nothing whatsoever to gain by saying anything other than "this book makes a fundamental contribution to an important field of study, so publish it." Happily, Elizabeth had written a very good book, so they were tempted to say nothing else.

So much for Panderbilt UP. Now let's turn to Panderbilt Books or "PB" as its known in the industry. PB is a trade press, that is, it produces books for a large market and hopes to make a profit on every one of them. PB pursues this objective, first of all, by being very choosy about the books it publishes. PB will not publish a book, as a university press might, simply because it makes a mighty contribution to what humanity needs to know to prosper in these troubled times. It's not that the people who run trade presses aren't interested in publishing what humanity needs to know; many of them—and especially the ones that publish serious popular history—are very concerned with humanity. It's just that trade presses, unlike university presses, are not subsidized by taxpayers' dollars, students' tuition, or donors' donations. They operate in the free market. This means they have to publish books that sell or turn the lights off. In order to get books that sell efficiently, they pursue a two-pronged strategy.

First, they use agents to do some of the choosing for them. If, on the one hand, an unknown historian sends a manuscript to a trade press editor, that editor will promptly throw it in the enormous slush pile of unsolicited submissions. Maybe an unpaid intern will look at it, maybe not. In either case, that's usually that for the manuscript. If, on the other hand, a well-respected agent "walks a book in" to an editor he knows personally, that's a different story entirely. The editor knows that said agent only "walks in" the good stuff, that is, stuff she knows she might be able to sell. From the editor's point of view, the agent has essentially saved her from the dreaded slush pile by making a first cut of books her firm might profitably publish. So instead of endlessly searching for a literary needle in a haystack, all the editor has to do is go to lunch with the pitch-ready agent. The editor may or may not buy a good history book, but she will certainly get a good meal.

Second, trade presses commission history books. Many would-be popular historians think that because they consider a subject interesting, other people will too. Sometimes they are right, but most of the time they are wrong. In contrast, the editors at trade presses know, more or less, what people who read history find interesting: war, biographies, politics, etc. They will, therefore, cut right to the chase and try to find historians who will write the books that they think will sell, namely, ones about war, notable individuals, and politics, etc. Sometimes the editor herself will reach out to popular historians. More frequently, the editor will call an agent or two and ask, "You know what I'd like to see on my desk? A book about the history of battleships. With big guns. Really big guns. Do you have anyone who can write that?" The agent will then make inquiries, hoping to find just such a hungry popular historian. From the historian's point of view, a commission is often much better than writing a book on spec, for it means he will be paid no matter what.

However a trade press happens to get a book it wants to publish, it will, after making the decision, take a keen interest in what's inside that book. An editor at a university press will almost never tell a professor what to say or how to say it in a book; academic authors, being very prideful people, don't respond kindly to this sort of direction from un-credentialed amateurs. A trade press editor, though, will feel no compunction about telling a signed and therefore partially paid author what to do in her book. The editor has to make sure the book will sell, and that means riding the author. If the author gets all snooty about being ridden, the editor can get out the editorial riding crop—the threat that she will "kill" the book and thereby deprive the author of a considerable amount of money.

Do not get the impression that this sort of literary negotiation is a bloody affair. On the contrary, it's usually very civil because the interests of the editor and the trade paperback history writer are closely aligned. They both want to produce a bestseller and cash in, among other things. If that entails ginning up this, toning down that, and sprinkling dramatic prose throughout, so be it. It's no sin to dim the lamp a bit so as to make it burn longer. If all goes well, the final product of this editorial back-and-forth will be a very readable history book on a very popular topic. True, it will not be as reliable as a monograph from a university press, and academic historians will probably turn their noses up at it. The editor cares about this not one bit. The author, who may have once wanted to be a history professor, cares a bit more. Neither of them will care two bits once the book begins to sell and the money rolls in.

Turning the title page, you will see another with a mass of

very fine print on it. As with most fine print, this is the work of lawyers. The page tells you stuff you don't want to know: where the press is headquartered, where its branch offices are, that "Panderbilt" is a registered trademark, and other such attorney bait. The climax of this "narrative" is a stern warning:

In other words, "DON'T EVEN TRY TO USE THIS BOOK TO MAKE MONEY OR WE'LL SUE YOUR PANTS OFF!" This is not an empty threat; if it's a big press, it has the lawyers to do it. That said, most presses rarely have to take anyone to the legal woodshed because they don't generally produce the kinds of things people like to copy illegally for redistribution. There's just no money in pirating dense history monographs or even popular history books. Most historians wish there were.

Moving down the page a bit, you encounter the "Library of Congress Cataloging-in-Publication Data." As a rule, all most people need to know about a book is what it's about. If, however, you are a librarian, you need to know a lot more. Happily, "LC"—as the Library of Congress is called in the trade—provides it and the publishers print it on the sixth page (or so) of every book they issue. The purpose of the cataloging information is to make every book uniquely identifiable and easily findable. To make sure no book is mistaken for any other, LC uses two devices: the book's very own ISBN (see above) and a set of other identifiers such as author, title, publisher, date of publication, and suggested call-number. To make sure you can find the book among all other books, LC places the tome within an astoundingly vast set of subject headings. For example, Elizabeth's book might be catalogued as "1. Feminism. 2. Feminism—United States. 3. Feminism—United States—Higher Education," with each header "catching" fewer books than the last. Since books are often about more than one thing, *From Young Ladies to Wild Womyn* might also be catalogued like this: "1. United States. 2. United States—History. 3. United States—History—Feminism," again, with the book catchment becoming narrower and narrower. This subject-heading system is, for good or ill, rapidly being made redundant by word-searchable electronic books. It's often far easier and more efficient to search a large database of books for certain key words than it is to try to navigate your way through LC's maze of subject headers. The former is like asking a book what it is about; the latter is like asking a librarian what they *think* a book is about.

The next page may or may not be blank. If not, it may contain an epigraph. An epigraph is essentially a little riddle in the form of a quote, usually by a well-known someone. With it, the author is asking, "Given everything you know about this book and its subject, dear reader, what do you think this means?" Sometimes epigraphs are impossible to figure out as they seem to bear no relationship at all to anything in the book—literary scholars like this sort of thing. Others are impossible to figure out because they are in foreign languages the reader doesn't know—historians, alas, favor this sort of thing. Most epigraphs, however, are pretty easy to understand. In history, the classic and the most clichéd is George Santayana's: "Those who cannot remember the past are condemned to repeat it." It means, of course, "This is really important so pay attention." More frequently, epigraphs are quotes from historical figures mentioned in the book saying something clever, portentous, or deep. Here's the one Elizabeth chose for her book: "'I never wanted to burn my bra.'—WLA member Paula Linkson, 1972." Elizabeth won't say why she selected that quotation because she knows guessing is the fun part.

If you don't see an epigraph, you may see a dedication. A cynic might say that every word in a history book is an opportunity for the historian to curry favor. But even a cynic would have to admit that the dedication is often an exception to this rule. It is the one place where the reader can be reasonably sure that the writer is telling the whole truth and nothing but the truth. As we've seen, historians suffer when writing history books. It should be added that they do not suffer alone. Their advisors suffer, their families suffer, and their friends suffer as well. The dedication is an opportunity for the historian to acknowledge and, perhaps, apologize for the pain their historical mania has inflicted on those they love. "For George, with love" is only four words, but it "says" (as they say) a whole heck of a lot about the writer and her relationship to George. Elizabeth's dedication runs: "For my parents, Jerry and Katherine Ranke, who supported me through thick and thin." She cried when she wrote it.

Falling hard on the heels of the epigraph or dedication, you'll see a page called "Contents." It's a table with two columns, one for titles of the book's subsections and one for the page numbers on which those subsections begin. The rows of the table are divided into three parts, though none of these parts have headers. They are the "front-matter" (the stuff before the chapters), the "body" (the chapters), and the "back-matter" (the stuff after the chapters). There is no hidden meaning in any of this, though there is one thing that we should perhaps explain because it is so bizarre—pagination. The most intuitive way to paginate a book is to choose a single number style and use it to number sequentially every physical page in the book from front to back. That way the eighty-sixth page in the physical book would have the number "86" printed somewhere on it. If you look at the right-hand column of the table of contents, you'll see that modern publishers are not really interested in intuition. Here they follow tradition, even where it makes no sense. Instead of one number style, they usually use two: Roman for the front-matter and Arabic for everything else. Instead of counting every page between the covers, they only count pages that they think should count: the very first "leaf" in the book, for example, is omitted from page calculations. Instead of printing a number on every page, they follow a strange convention by which the first page of every section remains without a page number. This final habit is particularly weird in view of the fact that the table of contents itself uses page numbers to tell the reader where sections begin, though the initial pages of those sections have no page numbers printed on them.

We should perhaps pause here to discuss chapter titles. As a rule, historians compose chapter titles in the same way they compose the short titles of the books they are in. The general intent is to say something suggestive of what's inside, but not too suggestive. If the chapter title is punchy and arresting, all the better. Elizabeth knows this convention very well. The first chapter of her book is about the emergence of radical feminism at the University of Westcostia, Priestly, 1961–1964. She does not, however, call that chapter: "The Emergence of Radical Feminism at the University of Westcostia, Priestly, 1961–1964." No one would. Instead, she calls it: "The Beginning." This is a terrific chapter title: short, evocative, and mysterious, while also hinting at what the chapter is about. It's so good that she uses it as a template for the remaining chapter titles: "The Hard Years," "The Rising," "The Backlash," "The End." Of course, if all you had was the table of contents, you'd have absolutely no idea what Elizabeth's book or any of its chapters were about. But that's not a problem, because if you have the table of contents, you probably have the book.

Next up, the preface. Some historians include them and others don't. They all should, for the preface gives them an opportunity to tell the author something of cardinal importance: why they wrote the book and why the reader should read it. As we've noted, history books do not fall out of the sky. They are written by flesh-and-blood individuals like Elizabeth Ranke, people who tortured themselves simply to understand a bit of the past. The reason they did so is directly related to the book they wrote; you cannot understand that book unless you know why they wrote it. This is crystal clear in the case of *From Young Ladies to Wild Womyn*. In the preface Elizabeth tells the story of how she discovered her mother's archive of radical feminist newspapers, how she was surprised by what she found there, and how she began to wonder what impact the university-based radical feminist movement had on the lives of contemporary women. In short, she tells you why the subject matters to her and, by extension, why it should matter to you. In a lessor known passage, George Santayana wrote, "Those who forget to read the preface will never understand what follows." Actually, he didn't, but he should have.

What usually follows is a section called "Acknowledgements." The purpose of this part of a history book has changed over time, particularly in academic history books. Once, when faculty jobs in history were rather easier to come by than they are today, the acknowledgements were a place to say "Thanks" to people who had contributed directly and significantly to the production of the book. In this era, acknowledgements were nothing more than a short list beginning, "The author would like to acknowledge the assistance of X, Y, and Z." Now, however, nervous historians use them essentially to establish, consolidate, and expand their professional networks in the hopes that some mutual backscratching will be done. They have, as a consequence, grown into long essays in which authors express fulsome gratitude to pretty much everyone they can think of who had anything to do with them or the book. As before, direct and significant contrib-utors—advisors, librarians, archivists, editors—are mentioned. But so are undergraduate classmates, fellow graduate students, faculty colleagues, anonymous reviewers, academic departments, journal editors, administrators, universities, foundations, institutes, friends, family members, drinking buddies, and baristas at the author's favorite coffee shop. It's not uncommon for the acknowledgements in academic history books to run several full pages and include well over 100 proper names. The profusion of contributors has made it difficult to figure out who really contributed to the book and who is just being given a polite nod. Ever mindful of her seemingly tenuous pre-tenure position, Elizabeth made sure she mentioned everyone who could possibly matter. Her acknowledgements covered three pages and made special note of the role her cat, Clio, played in the writing of *From Young Ladies to Wild Womyn*.

Turning the page, you may well see a list of maps and illustrations. If you do, you're lucky, because some history-book publishers have decided that these materials are not worth the price of reproduction. Trade-book editors are more likely to include them, largely because they know the reading public likes maps and illustrations. In contrast, university press editors are more likely to include as few as possible because they know the public will never see their $90 book on the history of migrant labor in nineteenth-century Westcostia. But if the book is fortunate enough to have "plates" (as they are called in the trade), they are probably not going to be very good. There was a time, long ago now, in which history books often had very elaborate fold-out maps and beautiful pictures. Not anymore. The maps found in most modern history books are almost cartoonish. One hesitates to call many of them maps at all; they are more like sketches of maps. As for images, they are usually badly rendered and poorly reproduced. The reason, of course, is money, or the lack thereof. Professional cartographers and photographers cost a lot of it. Presses—and especially university presses—don't have much of it. So it has now become common for editors to ask the authors to provide all the plates themselves. Historians are historians, not cartographers or photographers, so the results are typically of the "good enough" kind: not professional, but sufficient if you keep your standards in check. For her part, Elizabeth was wise enough not to take on the task herself. She asked a graphic designer—a friend from college, as it happened—to make a map of the Priestley campus and to repair some grainy old photos of demonstrations. The results were slightly better than "good enough," though she was disappointed when her editor told her that she could only include four photos in the book.

It is not unusual to find two other technical items in the proximity of the list of plates. The first item is a list of abbreviations. Historians generally write about people, and it is convenient that people generally have short names. They can easily be abbreviated by using the last name alone. So in *From Young Ladies to Wild Womyn*, Elizabeth refers to the radical feminist leader Catherine Comstock as "Comstock." But historians also frequently write about institutions, and these, alas, often have very long names. Elizabeth has to find a way to talk about the "Radical Feminist Revolutionary Cooperative" without having to write "Radical Feminist Revolutionary Cooperative" every time she does so. That would be very tiresome. So she abbreviates the name to "RFRC" and tells you so in the list of abbreviations at the front of the book. The fact that you keep forgetting what RFRC stands for and, therefore, have to refer repeatedly to the list of abbreviations at the front of the book is also tiresome. But what can be done?

The second technical item you may encounter in the front of a history book is a note on dating and/or language. Many historians write about times and places where people didn't figure time or write in the scripts we do. For example, the people who wrote the Old Testament didn't do either. So we read in 2 Kings 25: 8–9:

וּבַחֹדֶשׁ הַחֲמִישִׁי, בְּשִׁבְעָה לַחֹדֶשׁ--הִיא
שְׁנַת תְּשַׁע-עֶשְׂרֵה שָׁנָה, לַמֶּלֶךְ נְבֻכַדְנֶאצַּר
מֶלֶךְ-בָּא נְבוּזַרְאֲדָן רַב :בָּבֶל-טַבָּחִים, עֶבֶד
מֶלֶךְ בָּבֶל--יְרוּשָׁלָם

וַיִּשְׂרֹף אֶת-בֵּית-הֹנָה וְאֶת ,יְ-בֵּית הַמֶּלֶךְ
כָּל וְאֵת-בָּתֵּי יְרוּשָׁלַם וְאֶת-כָּל-בֵּית גָּדוֹל, שָׂרַף
בָּאֵשׁ

Now you probably can't read this because it's written in Hebrew script in the Hebrew language. If you could, you might translate it like this:

> Now in the fifth month, on the seventh day of the month, which was the nineteenth year of king Nebuchadnezzar, king of Babylon, came Nebuzaradan the captain of the guard, a servant of the king of Babylon, unto Jerusalem.
>
> And he burnt the house of the LORD, and the king's house; and all the houses of Jerusalem, even every great man's house, burnt he with fire.

But when, exactly, was the "fifth month, on the seventh day of the month, which was the nineteenth year of king Nebuchadnezzar?"

In order to answer that question, you have to know how the ancient Hebrews figured time and when Nebuchadnezzar ruled—both of which, as it turns out, are rather mysterious and subject to conflicting interpretations. The historian's job is not so much to decide which of these interpretations is correct as to tell you which one she used to convert old dates into new dates so you can understand when things happened from your point of view (probably 587 BCE in the present case). Similarly, the historian has to find a way to make the name of the king of Babylon נְבֻכַדְנֶאצַּר legible to you since you can't read Hebrew script. To do this, she has to know something about the way Ancient

Hebrew was pronounced—again, a rather mysterious subject open to conflicting interpretations. Among all the competing "transliteration systems," the author just has to pick one, tell you which, and stick with it throughout the book. Obviously, Elizabeth has no "Note on Dates and Transliteration" section in her book because her very modern subjects used the Gregorian Calendar and Latin letters.

So much for the throat-clearing portion of a history book. Now, some seven to ten pages into the presentation, the historian will begin to talk about the matter at hand. She will not, however, begin to tell you the story, for there is one more preliminary to be dealt with before the tale can be spun: the introduction. Ideally, historians will use the introduction to do two things.

The first is to set the scene. Time, at least as we reckon it, is constant and continuous: it goes backwards and forwards unendingly at the same velocity without any natural breaks. We impose order on time with devices like clocks and calendars. The past—meaning everything that has happened to objects in time heretofore—is variable and discontinuous. Things change more rapidly in one period than another, and indeed some things become other things over time. Some times have more history, while others less history. Historians impose order on the past with a device called "periodization," or the division of the past into eras that are both coherent—having a common set of characteristics—and distinct—different from the eras that preceded them and followed them. Without having ever read any history book, you may know some of the periods historians have carved out of the past, for example, Pre-History, The Ancient World, The Middle Ages, The Early Modern Period, and The Modern Period.

These periods, it's important to point out, are conventions; they are not written on the stars. They are not, however, entirely arbitrary. Rather, historians arrive at them by continuously and collectively comparing what they know about the past and what they think is important about the past. The former—knowledge about the past—is not arbitrary at all: a historical fact is a historical fact no matter whether it is acknowledged as such or not. It happened that way or didn't, full stop. The latter—the assignment of significance—is somewhat arbitrary, but not completely so. It's true, as the adage has it, that there is no accounting for taste. But the assignment of importance to a historical phenomenon is not just a matter of taste. Rather, it's a matter to be negotiated by everyone interested in history. You don't get to decide alone; you have to convince other people that it's important. In addition to fundamental research, that is, the discovery of new facts, this ongoing, never-ending, and sometimes remarkably frustrating negotiation is an important part of the historian's job. Sometimes a general consensus is reached, especially about the biggest periods like Pre-History and such. But much of the time it's not, and the historians simply keep arguing with one another about which periods are in fact periods given what we know. This is why history has to be constantly rewritten: we know more and the negotiation as to importance reaches a different equilibrium.

In the introduction, then, the historian should tell you how they divide history up and where the story they are about to tell you fits, period-wise. If they are writing in a very dogmatic tradition, like Marxism, they may do this explicitly. In the Soviet Union, for example, the Party told historians to use a standard Marxist periodization based on "modes of production," for example, The Antique Mode of Production, The Feudal Mode of Production, The Capitalist Mode of Production, and The Socialist Mode of Production. The Party then divided these macro-periods into smaller chunks, say early, middle, and late. In the introduction to every Soviet history book, the author had to place his or her story on this well-delineated timeline, or else.

Modern historians like Elizabeth are much more cagey about where their stories fit. In fact, they usually provide only a brief and quite vague sense of what came before their stories begin.

They do this because they themselves don't care much about the big picture nor do they probably know much about it. As we've seen, the overwhelming trend since the introduction of the German model in history has been toward specialization. As historians have brought the trees—indeed, the microscopic bugs on the trees—into sharper and sharper focus, the forest has all but vanished. Elizabeth knows a lot about late twentieth-century American history. She knows a bit less about pre-war American history, nineteenth-century American history, and Colonial American history. Her knowledge of every other historical epoch is that of a well-trained history major. She knows her stuff, not anyone else's. Needless to say, then, when she placed the story of radical feminism into its historical context in the introduction to her book, that context was late twentieth-century American feminism.

The second thing historians do—or should do—in introductions is to sketch the book. According to a shop-worn formula, good essay writers should: "Tell 'em what you're going to tell 'em, tell 'em, and then tell 'em what you told 'em." The same goes for history books, and most historians know that. A careful, chapter-by-chapter summary of a book can whet the reader's appetite for all the goodness that is to come. Moreover, it can also save the reader time by telling him what's in the book and what's not with a slightly higher level of accuracy than the table of contents. Finally, the summary could be used by someone—say an overworked graduate student—to suggest to someone else—say a comps committee member—that one has read an entire book when one actually has not. But no one would ever do that.

Having completed the introduction, the author begins to tell the reader in detail what he discovered in his research. This material, of course, is presented in chapters, or sometimes sets of chapters. Historians arrange the chapters in one of two ways: thematically or chronologically. If thematically, the historian's presentation will be like that of an anatomist describing the parts of a dead body, except he'll be talking about things like race, gender, and class rather than livers, hearts, and spleens. An anatomist's report rarely makes compelling reading, and the same is often true of thematic history. The reason is this: neither tells stories with a beginning, middle, and end. Rather, they describe the way things were at a certain time and place. If those things are really interesting, then the book might grab your attention. One imagines, for example, that a lot of people would want to read a thematic book called *More Sex, Please: The Erotic Lives of Common People in Post-Revolutionary Utopistan*. If those things are not really interesting, then they are more likely to put you to sleep. It's hard to imagine who, other than a professional historian of Utopistan, would ever read a book called *More Food, Please: The Everyday Lives of Common People in Post-Revolutionary Utopistan*. Because popular historians try to write exciting, drama-filled books that people will read, they shy away from the thematic mode of exposition. Not so academic historians, at least those in certain subspecialties. Social historians, for example, love thematic history because what they study—namely, the everyday lives of common people—generally doesn't lend itself to narrative presentation. Even a historical ninja would have trouble telling a good story about the everyday consumptive habits of peasants, workers, soldiers, and sailors immediately after the Great Revolution in Utopistan. They were what they were, just as a dead man's liver is his liver, his heart his heart, and his spleen his spleen.

If the chapters are arranged chronologically, the historian is not an anatomist describing a dead body, but—to continue the analogy—a detective explaining how the body got dead. The crucial difference is, of course, change-over-time. The historian-as-anatomist is interested in the how the body is right now; the historian-as-detective is interested in how the body got the way it is right now. The former renders a description; the latter tells a story. Elizabeth knows that bodies have parts and so do stories.

Pretty much everyone agrees on the parts of a body. There is more debate—much of it ridiculously arcane—about the parts of a story, but it seems sensible to agree with Aristotle that they all have (or should have) a beginning, middle, and end. Historians obviously believe this to be true, for they use Aristotle's tripartite model to structure their presentations on two levels, the book-level and the story-level. Concerning the former, historians are often quite explicit, as one can see in the table of contents: intro-duction (beginning), chapters (middle), conclusion (end). Regarding the latter, they are much more secretive, but nonetheless one can usually see the influence of Aristotle in deed if not word.

Each chapter begins with the title, the meaning of which we've already discussed. Below the chapter title, you may or may not see another epigraph; we've already touched on the meaning of those as well. And then begins the chapter text itself. When academic historians write books, they generally try to do so in such a way as to make the chapters stand-alone, that is, such that they can be read profitably by themselves. They do this for two reasons. First, they hope to publish one or more of the chapters as articles in journals before the book itself is complete and published. Essentially, they want to get two bits of tenure-ready credit for the price of creating one. Since journal articles must be stand-alone, historians write their book chapters to be stand-alone insofar as possible. Elizabeth, for example, published her best chapter as an article in the prominent *Journal of Feminist History* and she didn't have to make many modifications to do so. The second reason historians write stand-alone chapters is that they realize many readers will not take the time to read the entire book; they will only be interested in the material in one chapter. Therefore, as a courtesy to such selective readers, they try to make the chapters stand on their own.

Since historians try to make their chapters into little expos-itory essays, they follow the general formula prescribed for all expository essays, namely, "Tell 'em what you're going to tell 'em, tell 'em, and then tell 'em what you told 'em." In other words, the form of the chapters usually mimics the form of the book as a whole: an introduction with a brief summary of what is to come; the exposition, often with titled subsections; and, finally, a conclusion with brief summary and look forward to the next chapter. Because chapters are much shorter than books, each of these sections is highly condensed. And just to make sure that no reader misses what's going on, many historians will use stereo-typed phrases to tell them. "As we have seen" in the chapter's introduction means "I'm now setting the scene for what is come." "As we will see" in the chapter's conclusion means "I'm telling you what is to come." This same introduction-body-conclusion structure can be found on lower levels of the text as well, for example in subsections and even paragraphs. In this way, the book, chapters, subsections, and paragraphs are, formally at least, a bit like those nested Russian dolls: each is like the other, only bigger or smaller.

After the chapters have run their course, you will often see a conclusion or sometimes an epilogue. Historians generally use the conclusion as a forum for reiterating their argument ("tell 'em what you told 'em") and, more importantly, to discuss the meaning of the story they have told. Most modern philosophers of history agree that history actually has no meaning in the sense of progress toward some transcendental goal. Some religions assign history this sort of meaning (Christianity) and some political movements do as well (Marxism), but historians trained in the German model by and large do not, at least on a grand scale. So you are not going to find Elizabeth explaining how the history of radical feminists in late twentieth-century America fits into some overarching, cosmic plan.

This is not to say that this history has no meaning for Elizabeth. It does, it's just of a different type than the kind intended by Christians and Marxists. Their meaning is universal, while her meaning—and that of other historians schooled in the German model—is local, that is, pertaining to her and those for whom she writes. As we've seen, Elizabeth is an American feminist historian who, though she might be interested in speaking to larger audiences, has in fact written a book for other American feminist historians. She is one of them and is speaking to them. It's not surprising, then, that whatever meaning she finds in the story she tells pertains to them. The question she addresses in her conclusion, then, is, "What does this story mean for us?" The answer, far from being abstract and speculative as you might imagine, is in fact rather concrete and technical. This is because what a story like Elizabeth's means to a group of scholars is, well, scholarly. Elizabeth's readers, academics all, want to know how what she says aligns with the received view, where that view is wrong, and what needs to be changed in it as a result of her research. In the conclusion, Elizabeth will tell them. "My research shows so-and-so, therefore we now have to revisit this, that, and the other established truth." For Elizabeth and her peers, that is the meaning of *From Young Ladies to Wild Womyn*.

As a rule, the conclusion is followed by the book's "back-matter," the first bit of which may be an appendix or two if the book is published by a university press. Historians generally use appendices to present technical material they could not shoehorn into the text for whatever reason. Examples include: primary documents, tabular data, genealogies, notes on statistical methods, and so on. These items are rarely very interesting, though they may provide essential information for the case the author is making. Elizabeth included two appendices in her book: a transcript of a seminal manifesto written, collectively of course, by the Women's Liberation Army and a year-by-year list of the membership of the WLA's Central Committee.

The notes follow the appendices, if any. In a former age, the notes would have been found at the bottom of the pages to which they pertain, in other words, they would have been "footnotes." Alas, that day is gone. For reasons that are beyond comprehension, even university presses now place the notes at the back of their books; this is why they are sometimes and rightly called "endnotes." This regrettable practice of exiling the notes to the end of a book means that in order to look at a note pertaining to a certain sentence you have to find it in the back of the book. Since most people find this process of flipping back and forth wearisome, they don't look at the notes at all. And that is the saddest part of the story of notes, because the notes contain material that is absolutely essential for understanding a history book.

The notes are where the author tells you how he knows what he claims he knows. They are, if not the evidence for his case itself, pointers to that evidence. Historians generally write three kinds of notes: citations, bibliographic notes, and discursive notes. A citation points the reader to a specific primary or secondary source and, if well-formed, a specific place in that item, say a folio or page. With a citation, the historian is saying: "It says this, verbatim or in effect, here." Normally citations include nothing but the information necessary to identify the source as it is found in the list of sources or bibliography of the book. A bibliographic note points the reader to one or more secondary sources where the topic at hand is discussed. With a bibliographic note, the historian is saying, "If you want to know more about this, look here." The author will frequently feel the need to guide the reader through a bibliographic note, particularly if it contains multiple items. So you might read, "On this, see…", "On that, see…" and "On the other thing, see…" all in the same bibliographic note. A discursive note provides clarification about something in the text. With a discursive note, the historian is saying, "Here's some more of my thinking on that." Discursive notes are often several sentences long and can, if one is not careful, turn into little essays. Since most historians believe all important discussions should be in the text itself, discursive notes are generally considered bad practice.

It remains to be said that the notes found in many popular history books are quite different from those found in academic histories. The editors at trade presses know that almost no one is going to look at the notes of a popular history book. History buffs generally want good stories, not proof that good stories meet professional standards of proof. For this reason, these editors will sometimes omit the notes entirely from a book. They would probably omit them more often were it not for the objections of the historians who write them. Some popular historians have PhDs in history, so they want notes in their books. Other popular historians want academics to pay attention to their work, so they also want notes in their books. In the end, the editors and popular historians usually compromise: the book has notes, but of a peculiar sort. In such cases, the text itself has no superscripted numeric note-references; in fact, it has no indication that there are notes at all. Rather, the reader is left to guess which sentences on any given page have a note attached to them in the "Notes" section in the back of the book. That section is not arranged by note number, for there are no note numbers. Instead, it's arranged by page and sentence within the page. To indicate which sentence a note refers to, the publisher prints the first few words of the sentence in question. Needless to say, this system of reference is so confusing and clumsy as to render the notes themselves practically useless. From the editor's perspective, of course, that's fine, for the notes aren't meant to be used at all. They are window-dressing.

The bibliography falls after the notes in most history books. Alas, sometimes it doesn't fall anywhere at all: it's increasingly the case that trade presses and sometimes even academic presses omit bibliographies entirely. In the case of trade presses, this is perhaps understandable: very few readers are going to look at the bibliography of a popular history. In the case of academic presses, it's absolutely baffling: academic readers love bibliographies and use them all the time. In many history books, the bibliography will be divided into sections, for example, one for archival sources, another for printed primary sources, and a third for secondary sources. Archival sources are arranged in alphabetical order by the name of the archive (e.g. "Priestly Municipal Archive"), the location, a file in the archive ("Section 83; Division C"), and the name of the file ("Investigation of the Women's Liberation Army, 1967–68"). Only experts can decode these sorts of entries, but then again they are intended for experts. Printed primary sources and secondary sources are arranged by the last name of the editor or author. It's worth mentioning that bibliographies, particularly in academic books, have become incredibly bloated. Looking through them one can find all kinds of material that is, seemingly, completely unrelated to the topic of the book. This bibliographic inflation is due to two things: the expansion of the literature—there's just more stuff to cite—and the growing anxiety authors feel about leaving anyone who might matter out. One of the first things any historian does when he gets a new book is look in the bibliography to see if his work is there. It better be.

The final section of a history book is—or rather should be—the index. As with the notes and bibliography, however, the index has now become optional. Publishers just don't want to pay to have books indexed. Instead, they ask authors to do it. As anyone who has read Kurt Vonnegut's *Cat's Cradle* will know, there are myriad reasons not to index your own book. One of them is that it takes a lot of time—time most authors would rather spend basking in the glory of their newly published books. Another is that it takes some skill, and authors—especially first-time authors—are hardly indexing mavens. Finally, even if an author indexes his book, the publisher might decide not to print it just to save some money. Given all this, it's not surprising that publishers have a bit of trouble convincing authors to take up the task. Most, however, do, though the results are a mixed bag. On the one hand, at least there is an index. On the other hand, it's probably not a very good one: names are missing, subjects are absent, page numbers wrong, etc. Elizabeth, for example, found that indexing her book was an excruciating process. Not only was the work deadly boring, but she was constantly wracked by the feeling she was missing something. As it turned out, she was: her advisor's name—which appears several times in the text—is not to be found in the index. Elizabeth is absolutely sure she'll notice.

Enough about the sundry parts of a modern history book. Let us now turn to another important concern: the hidden parts of history books.

Chapter 6

Some Things Hidden in History Books

The best parts of history books are the ones that aren't there.
—Reinhardt Friedrich Freiherr von Teufel

Elizabeth Ranke, now professor, has been wondering about the dance of thought and expression. She was prompted to do so after she began to see, very dimly at first, that the two were intertwined in her own writing. She recognized that she had fit her thoughts about radical feminists in the 1960s into a kind of template, that is, into the manifest parts of a modern history book. This did not bother her; after all, she knew exactly what she was doing when she applied the template. She used it; it didn't use her. Yet she also began to suspect that she had quite unintentionally fit her thoughts about radical feminism in the 1960s to another kind of template, one that was essentially hidden behind the manifest parts. This bothered her a lot; for here she didn't know what she was doing when she unknowingly applied it. She didn't use it; it used her. And this thought led her to another, even more disturbing one: "Could it be," she asked herself, "that there are messages hidden in my writing, messages that I put there but did not know I was putting there?" This was a topic worth considering. So, late on a chilly winter afternoon after a long day at the office, Elizabeth settled into an overstuffed chair with her cat Clio on her lap and began to think precisely about choices she made but did not make, about the messages she sent but did not send.

Elizabeth brings *From Young Ladies to Wild Womyn* to mind. In that book, Elizabeth told the story of collegiate feminists in the 1960s: who they were, what they did, and why they did it. The story was based on hard evidence: documents, transcripts, letters, memoirs, reports, and other primary sources found in libraries and archives. She didn't make it up. She found the story in the sources. She didn't write the story; the story wrote itself. The image of a pen magically dancing across a sheet of paper appears in her head. "That's absurd," she thinks, "stories don't write themselves. People write them, people like me." This doesn't really upset her until she recalls that people—people like her—have agendas even when they aren't supposed to. According to the German model, historians are supposed to write history *sine ira et studio*. That is a fine ideal, and a goal that most historians strive toward and to a considerable extent achieve. But only to a considerable extent. Upon reflection, Elizabeth realizes that there is always a bit of an agenda hidden behind every history, even her own. This is a troubling idea. She begins to consider whether it might be late enough in the day to have a drink.

But before she can settle the question as to what to quaff (white or red?), a more unnerving query pops into her head: "What was my hidden agenda?" It seemed pretty obvious. She's a feminist, she is interested in feminists, and she thinks the world should know about feminists. That's why she chose to study the history of feminism. "That's all well and good," she thinks, "but it doesn't mean I skewed the history of Priestly's feminists in the 1960s to fit my own designs. I told the story as I found it in the sources. Given the sources, there was no other way to tell the story other than the way I told it. It's just what happened." In Elizabeth's telling, "what happened" was that the early Priestly feminists, her protagonists, came to consciousness through socialism in the early 1960s; they then met and struggled with various antagonists—conservative students, university administrators, politicians; and, finally, they succeeded in convincing most everyone that female students should be treated the same as male students.

Elizabeth decides on a nice Riesling. Besides, the bottle was already open. She displaces Clio, heads to the kitchen, pours herself a hefty glass, and returns to her comfy chair and her musings. "It really is impossible to tell the story any other way," Elizabeth assures herself. "Everyone believes in feminism, and everyone believes that the Priestly feminists were brave pioneers." She takes a sip of wine and thinks about what "everyone" thinks. It's true that pretty much everyone Elizabeth knows believes that feminism is a good thing, and therefore pretty much everyone Elizabeth knows would think the feminists at Priestly were heroines if they would take the time to read her book. Pity, she thinks, they won't.

And then, suddenly, the image of Russ Doubtless appears in her consciousness. She hasn't thought of Russ in decades. Elizabeth went to college with him. They lived on the same floor in Hurlchunk Hall when they were freshmen. She never much liked him. He didn't drink, do drugs, and he really believed in God. Rumor had it that Russ was a member of some wacky religious cult. And Russ certainly was no feminist, as she learned during one of those endless, frothy discussions freshmen have about big questions in the dining hall. Russ, it seemed, didn't think abortion should be allowed under any circumstance. It was murder plain and simple, he said. Needless to say, Elizabeth had nothing to do with Russ and his awful opinions after freshman year. In fact, she had totally blotted him out of her mind.

Until now. "What if," she asks herself, "Russ had written the history of radical feminism at Priestly in the 1960s? Would he have told the story in the same way I did?" A number of years ago, Elizabeth would have thought so. If Russ was trained in the German model, if he looked at all the same materials she had, and if he had written a university-press style book for a university press in the hopes of getting tenure, then the stories should be roughly the same. After all, what happened is what happened. But, she realizes, the stories really would have been different. Russ would tell the reader how his protagonists, the traditional Christian women at Priestly, came to consciousness through campus Bible study in the early 1960s; how they met and struggled with various antagonists—radical feminists, university administrators, politicians; and how, in the end, they failed to convince most people that female students should be treated differently than male students. He would probably also claim, as Elizabeth had, that there was no other way to tell the story. What happened is what happened.

Elizabeth pours herself another glass of wine and coaxes Clio back on her lap. "I didn't mean to skew the story of Priestly's feminists, I really didn't. I wanted to write a true story. I really did. What happened?" The first thing that occurs to her is that she did write a true story insofar as she didn't make anything up. Every factual claim she made in *From Young Ladies to Wild Womyn* was true and could be verified by reference to the primary sources. The same, of course, could be said of Doubtless' seemingly very different story—it, too, would have been true in that narrow sense. "How," she wonders, "could there be two true stories about the same things?" To answer that question, more wine was required.

She sits and thinks, stroking Clio. Upon finishing her third glass of wine, she sees it: the subjects are the same, but the stories are different. What happened in Priestly in the 1960s is what happened. The moment it happened it was fixed and could not be changed. But the story of what happened can vary. Most people think of stories in terms of their content, what they are "about": this story is *about* radical feminists in the 1960s. But actually the content is just the surface of a story. The container of that "content" is not just a generic, one-size-fits-all story, but a kind of story. Without any recourse to fancy literary theory, we all know this: some kinds of stories have "happy endings" and some kinds of stories have "sad endings." The fancy literary critic would say that the former is "plotted" like a comedy, while the latter is "plotted" like a tragedy. But no matter what you call them, they are kinds of stories. And, significantly, a skilled author—or, in our case, historian—can pour pretty much any content into the one or the other story-mold, no matter what that content may be. The facts are determined by the sources, as Elizabeth knows. But the kind of story one uses to makes those facts meaningful is not. That is determined in the main by what the story means to the storyteller, which is to say their values. Elizabeth is a feminist so she tells the story of what happened in Priestly in the 1960s as a triumph over adversity. Doubtless is conservative so he tells the story of what happened in Priestly in the 1960s as a tragedy. Neither of them was fully conscious of what they were doing when they poured the content into the story-mold. It just seemed natural.

"Christ," she thinks, "I'm a fraud and a hack. We're all frauds and hacks. We tell everyone that we're telling stories as they actually happened, but in fact we're spinning the stories according to our own agendas. And the worst part of it is we often don't realize we're doing it at all." This sobering thought moves Elizabeth to switch from white wine to corn whiskey, a taste for which she acquired back when she lived cheek-by-jowl with the distasteful Russ Doubtless. Once again Clio is ejected as she hops up to pour herself a tumbler of booze, neat. Back in her comfy chair, glass in hand and cat back in lap, Elizabeth reconsiders. She's being too hard on herself. She's not really a hack and a fraud. She did the best she could to tell it like it was, and she's pretty sure most historians do the same. Stories have plots; plots are partial. That's just the cost of doing historical business. She's concerned, however, that further consideration of kinds of stories and degrees of bias will drive her further to drink. So she lets her mind wander to another message hidden in her writing.

For a second time, Elizabeth brings *From Young Ladies to Wild Womyn* to mind. So what, she thinks, if she didn't tell *the* story of feminism at Priestly? She told a story, and it was a heck of a good one. Those women were way ahead of their time, and everyone could learn a lot from them. Take Annabelle Blanc. Elizabeth devoted an entire section of the book to her. She was a real heroine. She grew up in dire poverty in rural Owlabama. Her father abandoned the family and soon after her mother married an abusive alcoholic who, well, abused her. She helped raise her eleven brothers and sisters in their doublewide trailer. They often went hungry and barefoot. They walked ten miles to school, uphill both ways. She won a scholarship to Priestly in 1961 and there had her consciousness raised. She joined "Radical Action for Democracy" (RAD) and participated in numerous sit-ins, stand-ups, walkouts, and take-overs. The "swine" arrested her several times, though the food was pretty good "inside." In 1963 she left RAD because it was dominated by men. "Patriarchy will not prevail!" she shouted at a RAD meeting before exiting the hall with like-minded feminists. She then founded the "Women's Liberation Army" (WLA) and continued her fight for justice. Again, she and her confederates sat-in, stood-up, walked-out, and took-over. Again, the "swine" arrested her and served her tasty hot meals. As leader of the WLA, her greatest triumph was on what the feminists called the "Bathroom Front." She and her "sisters" occupied toilets, both male and female, all over campus. It was dirty work, but in the end the chancellor of the university conceded the WLA's chief demand: toilet equality. Blanc proved unable to hold the WLA together. In 1968, it dissolved into six factions (the RUP, FRE, SWE, QWE, NCT, and PIR). Blanc returned to Owlabama without finishing her degree, though she continued to fight for justice. She died in 2001 as a result of an Echinacea overdose.

Elizabeth, now somewhat tipsy, looks down at Clio and asks rhetorically: "Who wouldn't admire the pluck of that woman? I imagine even that bastard Doubtless would. He might not agree with what she did, but heck, she was a hell of a broad!" Clio stares back at her and, much to Elizabeth's surprise, says, "But she was an inveterate racist, Lizzy. She didn't like black folks one bit. That's hardly something you, Doubtless, or anyone else would admire." Elizabeth looked at the cat in amazement, trying to figure out if she was imagining things. "Must be the whiskey," she thinks. She takes another drink. She has to admit that the cat has a point. Blanc was indeed a racist. In her personal archive, Elizabeth had read a letter Blanc wrote to one of her siblings disparaging African Americans. "You wouldn't believe all the uppity negroes around here. They think they're better than white folks just because they go to college. I can understand they are proud of themselves, and that's fine. But they've got quite the nerve sitting in the front of bus and class. They don't know their place."

Elizabeth did not mention Blanc's attitudes on race in *From Young Ladies to Wild Womyn*. From her perspective, Blanc's views on the subject were irrelevant. Elizabeth's focus was on feminism at Priestly, not on what feminists might or might not have privately thought about issues like race relations. Truth be told, though, there were at least two pieces of evidence that suggested Blanc's racism might have had some impact on her public life. First, the Central Committee of the WLA never had an African American on it while Blanc was at its head. There could have been many reasons for that other than racial prejudice, Elizabeth thought, for example a lack of suitable candidates. Second, there was a student newspaper article that claimed Blanc had said whites and blacks should not really mix, but rather should be separate and equal. The author of this article, however, was a strident opponent of both Blanc and the WLA, Elizabeth recalled, so there was good reason not to credit it. The evidence that Blanc's racism affected her public actions, then, was both sketchy and suspect, therefore Elizabeth saw no reason to mention it in the book.

Elizabeth turned again to Clio: "See, you cursed cat, I wasn't hiding anything. That stuff about Blanc not liking blacks just wasn't German, or germane, or whatever that word is. I didn't deceive anyone." This time Clio said nothing in response, which eased Elizabeth's mind considerably. But Elizabeth wondered if she might have given the wrong impression by omitting to say that Blanc was a racist. She thought about. She had long ago noted that her undergraduates tended to fill in the blanks when it came to historical figures, and that they did not always do so correctly. If she presented someone in a lecture as holding opinion X, then her students would assume that this someone must have also held opinion Y because X and Y always "naturally" went together. This being so in their experience, the students projected the inevitable union of X and Y back in time, where, unfortunately, they were not united and did not belong.

The Great Liberator, Elizabeth thought, is the classic example of this form of anachronistic reasoning. He freed millions of black slaves, therefore—so the students inferred—he must have believed in racial equality. But he didn't. Exactly what the Great Liberator thought about blacks changed over the course of his long career, but he never suggested that they were equal to white people. On the eve of the Great Liberation itself he was seriously considering whether it might not be better if they were made to leave the country and live among their own "race." He held no animus against blacks, and it wouldn't be too much to say that he loved them as he loved all men. He just didn't think that blacks and whites were equal or that they should live together. He was the Great Liberator, emancipator-racist.

The example of Mary Singer then came to Elizabeth's mind. In her class on the history of sexuality, Elizabeth tells her students that Singer was a brave pioneer of birth control and therefore contributed mightily to the cause of women's liberation. And this, indeed, is how most historians and the public at large remember her. Few would doubt that the entire world owed her a great debt. But Elizabeth doesn't stop there, because she knows if she did she would give precisely the wrong impression of Singer and her times. Singer wasn't just a pioneer of birth control, she was also an advocate of eugenics. She believed that it was the duty of every progressive to "ensure the health of the race." Therefore it was only rational that the government should prevent those deemed "unfit" from reproducing in the interest of national well-being. She suggested selective sterilization. Elizabeth's students are always shocked to learn that Singer believed in both women's liberation and eugenics because for them these two ideas cannot go together. When they hear about advocates of birth control, they think of good, modern people like themselves. When they hear about selective sterilization programs, they think of the National Racists' Party, the group that perpetrated the Great Murderous Rampage during the Second Big War. For these undergraduates, Mary Singer is an impossibility, a remarkable progressive who was also of one mind with the hated NRP. Happily, Elizabeth is there to tell them that Singer was not an impossibility; in fact she was a very real progressive-eugenicist.

And now Elizabeth has another example of ideas that cannot be mixed but are in fact mixed: Annabelle Blanc, feminist-racist. "Crap," she says to Clio, "I think I blew it here." By not mentioning that Blanc held retrograde opinions about race, she afforded her readers the opportunity to fill in the blank. She knows just how they will do it, namely, by assuming that because Blanc was progressive in one way she was progressive in all ways, that she must have believed in both the equality of women and the equality of races. The truth is, though, she didn't believe any such thing.

Naturally Elizabeth didn't mean to give this impression, at least consciously. In *From Young Ladies to Wild Womyn*, she wanted to tell the truth, the whole truth, and nothing but the truth. But she had neither the time nor the space to tell the whole truth; she had a few years to write the story and a few hundred pages in which to tell it. Some things had to be left out. And besides, even if she had had both the time and the space to tell the whole story, it wouldn't have been much of a story. If you tell everything, you effectively tell nothing. Good stories are about focus, and when everything is told all focus is lost. Again, some things must be left out. The result is anachronism, but there is nothing one can do about that. Naturally this distresses Elizabeth to no end and she decided, once again, to move on to another unconscious choice and hidden message.

For a third time, Elizabeth brings *From Young Ladies to Wild Womyn* to mind. She's drunk, so her thoughts are cloudy. But she is also freed of inhibition and therefore ready to admit what she has known all along but never had the courage to say. She takes a drink, clears her throat, and addresses Clio: "You know, cat, a lot of what I wrote in *From Young Ladies to Wild Womyn* is complete and utter malarkey. I mean, entire sections make no good sense or say nothing of substance at all." And it's true, there are longish stretches in which Elizabeth seemed to have forgotten the basic rules of good expository writing. Her paragraphs have no topic sentences, bodies, or conclusions. Her sentences are so long, wordy, and grammatically complex that the reader gets totally lost in them. She habitually uses the passive voice, thereby making it difficult to figure out who did what. She routinely makes asides within sentences as if she's forgotten to tell you something. She not only fails to pick the right word, but chooses one that is flat out wrong. She writes "certainly," "doubtless," and "clearly" so frequently that one wonders if she's really sure at all. Similarly, she qualifies propositions with "perhaps," "maybe," and "might" so often that the reader gets the impression she's just guessing. And, when dealing with quantities, she is so ready to write "some," "many," and "most" that it's hard to imagine she knows how much of anything there really was.

"What the hell happened?" she asks Clio. "Am I a bad writer? Just tell me the truth, you goddamned cat, am I a bad writer? I'm a bad writer. I know it, I'm a bad writer!" She upends the glass of whiskey, hoping for some relief from this orgy of self-loathing.

Elizabeth, of course, is hardly alone in thinking that bad history writers are responsible for bad history writing. "Yes," your typical historian will say, "Professor Upchuck has some really good ideas. It's a shame she can't put two words together." The trouble with the bad-writers-write-bad-history thesis is, however, that it ignores the difference between literary writing and historical writing. Good novelists must have considerable literary talent because novels are more style than substance. In the hands of anyone but the preternaturally gifted Tolstoy, a novel set during the Napoleonic invasion of Russia would probably have been more of a disaster than the invasion itself. In contrast, good historians needn't have any special literary skill because history books are more substance than style. Almost any well-trained historian could write a serviceable history of the Napoleonic invasions of Russia if she had a good grasp of the material and the guidelines of expository writing.

Elizabeth thinks again. "Right. I may be a bad writer, as you say, you accursed cat. But that has nothing to do with it. Good history writing is not that hard. You don't need to be a great wordsmith. You just have to follow the rules." That's a comforting thought, but, alas, it prompts another less comforting one: "Hold on a second, you blasted furball. I thought I was following the rules! I know Strunk and White by friggin' heart. Yet I still produced intellectual oatmeal. What. The. Hell. Happened!" Clio, sensing Elizabeth's frustration and despair, jumps off her lap and runs out of the room. Elizabeth, now sulking, begins to think about what the hell happened. Yes, she thought she was following the rules of good exposition. But, she recalls, at certain points in the book they proved very hard to follow. Her thoughts just didn't fall into place as they should have. They seemed to resist proper form. "Why is that?" she asks herself.

She wobbles out of the room and brings back a well-worn copy of *From Young Ladies to Wild Womyn*. Clio follows. She turns to the places where she knows she was bullshitting, where she had stopped making good sense, where the paragraphs are malformed, the sentences are clumsy, and the word choice all wrong. These passages were scattered throughout the book, but one in particular draws her attention, the one where she attempted to "engage theory." She recalls that back in graduate school, all the smart people were "engaging theory." She wasn't quite sure why, but she suspected it was because historians seem to have a kind of science envy, that is, they wished history produced the kind of grand theories that disciplines like biology, physics, and chemistry do. Elizabeth, having taken some science classes in college, knew what a scientific theory was: a coherent set of empirically testable propositions that purports to explain a wide field of diverse phenomena. But the so-called theories her colleagues were "engaging" — and the ones she thought she should "engage" too — weren't theories in this sense at all. They were neither coherent nor testable. They were, however, chalk full of arcane, scientific-sounding jargon: "discourses," "inter-texts," "epistemes," "alterities", "simulacra," "hegemonies," "interstices" and such. She dutifully "deployed" these words in *From Young Ladies to Wild Womyn*, though she never really understood what they meant. It wasn't that she didn't try to think them through; rather, they could not be thought through. And because they could not be thought through, they could not be expressed in a way that any normal reader could comprehend.

And then it occurs to her. In every one of the places that she had written badly, she didn't really know what she wanted to say. Her mind rested between two stools, or perhaps three, or it found no stool at all. She was confused, vexed, baffled, or perplexed. She had not taken the time to think it — whatever it was — through, out or any other way. She turns to Clio: "Cat, I've figured it out. Bad history writers don't produce bad history writing. Bad thinking does." If, on the one hand, a historian has a clear and distinct idea of what she wants to say, then she will find it relatively easy to express it in good form. If, on the other hand, that historian is unclear about what she wants to say, then she will discover it is very hard to make it plain in any form. "Okay, okay, okay," Elizabeth says to Clio. "If I want to write better, I don't need to take writing classes. I just need to think better. But I can't do that right now, cat, because I'm hammered. I better go to bed."

And she does.

Chapter 7

What History Books are Good For

The truth is out there. If we're lucky, it's also in history books.
—Reinhardt Friedrich Freiherr von Teufel

Elizabeth Ranke, now retired professor, has been thinking about what history books are good for. For many years, the question never occurred to her. There was no need to ask it because everyone knew that history books were marvelous things. Not only were they often well-researched, beautifully written, attractively produced testaments to mankind's dogged pursuit of truth, they were also, so people said, miraculous instruments of enlightenment. Through their books, historians taught people about the past so they wouldn't have to repeat it. Thereby, historians and their books played an important role in human progress, that wondrous movement of mankind from imperfection to perfection. After all, those in the know proclaimed, if we don't know where we've been, then we may well be lost. If we're lost, then we won't know how to get where we're going. In short, the received wisdom was this: history books showed us the way into the bright future by showing us where we'd been in the dim past.

But Elizabeth doesn't buy the party line on history books anymore. She's not a cynic, but she's seen enough of the history industry to know that it doesn't really live up to its self-congratulatory billing. Some history books are indeed marvelous things. But many are poorly researched and badly executed. This unevenness is the result of haste. Newly minted PhDs rush to turn their manuscripts into books so that they can land tenure-track jobs or achieve tenure itself. The jobs are few, the competitors many, and so there is no time to waste on "thinking it through." The presses don't care much if a book is half-baked so long as they have a couple of positive blind but not really blind reviews in hand and a promise that a certain number of university libraries will buy it. As for being attractively produced, many—and especially those unjacketed monstrosities that university presses sell to university libraries at exorbitant prices—are just downright ugly. These hard-bound horrors are an insult to authors, readers, and book-designers everywhere.

Most disturbingly, history books most certainly are not engines of enlightenment, at least not effective ones. How could they be when only professional historians and geeky history buffs read them, and darned few of those? The unholy alliance between university presses and academic libraries has been spectacularly successful in delivering quality history books to this narrow slice of the citizenry. But it has completely failed to reach the public with this important material. This is true for many reasons, but the most obvious is that university presses and libraries do not seem to be able to think beyond that most beloved medium, text. Year in and year out, they try to sell—or say they are trying to sell—expensive history books to a public that wants history but has no taste at all for expensive history books. There is an enormous amount of video history on TV and the Internet. None of it is produced by university presses or professional historians. Millions upon millions of people watch video history on TV and the Internet. The university presses don't care and neither do most historians who write for the university presses.

"So," Elizabeth asks herself, "what good are history books?" There are some obvious things: they make the people who write them feel good about themselves, at least for a little while; they get lucky historians cushy jobs from which they cannot be fired for anything short of molesting undergraduates; they enable book publishers and retailers to put food on the table, though not much of it; they give historians something to argue about at annual conferences, though nobody outside those conferences gives a hoot; they provide photographers with impressive backdrops for scholarly portraits, though you could do that a lot less expensively with painted backdrops; they give browsers something to look at in bookstores, though there are fewer and fewer bookstores around; they provide thousands of tons of cellulose for useful things like insulation, adhesives, and textiles.

"I'm a cynic after all," Elizabeth mutters to herself. "There must be something else, some contribution that the history book industry makes to humanity." And then it occurs to her that there is, and it is a mighty contribution at that. History books do not prevent people from doing the same hurtful, ill-considered, crazy things they did in the past. If that were the case, there would be no war, poverty, oppression, etc. People are people, and it seems that no matter how many history books historians write and publishers publish, they will do the same hurtful, ill-considered, crazy things that people do. Over and over. Forever.

History books do, however, help prevent people from making stuff up about the past. Lunatics can deny that the Great Murderous Rampage happened, and they sometimes do. But only a few folks will believe them because historians have worked long and hard to find out not only if it happened, but also how it happened and why. They wrote their findings down in history books that anybody interested in the topic can read. These books are not hard to find, nor are they hard to get if you have a university library card or, say, $45; for that the university presses and libraries are to be warmly thanked. They are also very convincing insofar as they were written by historians, like Elizabeth, who were trained in the German model. They have footnotes, those footnotes cite sources, those sources can often be found in archives, and those archives are usually open for anyone to walk into. If the skeptical reader doesn't want to believe what someone like Elizabeth says about this or that fact, they can follow the well-marked trail that leads from a footnote in *From Young Ladies to Wild Womyn* to a file indexed and stored in a regrettably underfunded archive in the city of Priestly, Westcostia. There they can see for themselves. "Historians and their books," Elizabeth concludes, "constitute a kind of factual bulwark against historical bullshit."

That is a very valuable service, no doubt. Its value is readily apparent to anyone who has had the opportunity to study the way history was practiced in places like The Workers' Paradise and The Racists' Empire. Thanks to her excellent undergraduate and graduate education, Elizabeth has had this opportunity. So she knows this: upon seizing power in these two countries, the bosses of the Workers' Liberation Party (WLP) and the National Racists' Party (NRP) promptly fired, exiled, or killed all real historians. The party leaders dispatched them because they knew two things. First, they knew that true historians would write true stories about the past. That was politically inconvenient, for the WLP and NRP had things to hide from the public. Second, they knew that people would believe what these historians said because they had built credibility under their respective Old Regimes. That, too, was politically inconvenient, for the WLP and NRP wanted a monopoly on the people's trust. For the WLP and NRP, then, the course was clear: historians like Elizabeth had to be somehow muted. And they were.

The bosses of the WLP and the NRP were reasonably sophisticated people. They were not ready to do away with history altogether. That would have been uncivilized. They wanted, however, to use history to their own political ends. So they replaced the real historians with hacks and flacks, or rather hackish flacks, who would do their bidding. Their bidding was not to write true stories about the past, but to stoke resentments, resentments that were in fact the foundations of the Workers' Liberation and National Racist movements. Resentments, of course, are angry feelings about the past, a past in which somebody evil did something evil to you, or so you imagine. A resentment is like dog poop on your shoe; once it's there, you can't easily get rid of it. Resentments appear in your mind unbidden, frequently, and in all kinds of conditions. You might be eating lunch. It's tasty. And then there it is, your resentment. You might be watching the snow fall. It's beautiful. And then there it is, your resentment. You might be making love. It's blissful. And then there it is, your resentment. Everything, it seems, reminds you of the harm that someone evil did to you. And there is nothing you can do about it.

The WLP and NRP chiefs understood the incredible power of resentments and, more importantly for our purposes, they saw that historians and history books could be used to refine and amplify them for political ends. The resentments they were interested in stoking already existed, though they were vague and weak. The people of The Workers' Paradise, like all people, envied other people's wealth, so much so that they all knew a little story about it: "We are poor *because* they are rich." The people of The Racists' Utopia, like all people everywhere, feared strangers in their midst, so much so that they, too, all knew a little story about it: "We are afraid *because* they live among us." Though everyone knew these stories and occasionally took self-pitying comfort in them, no one took them too seriously.

No one, that is, outside the WLP and NRP. For some WLP and NRP members, these stories were not only true, they also spoke unequivocally about what had to be done if the nation were to achieve salvation, namely, get rid of the rich and the strangers. For other WLP and NRP members, however, the stories were just tools that might be useful in winning popular support. Both true believers and cynics in the respective parties, however, agreed that the stories offered wonderful opportunities for political gain if they could be refined and amplified. The people had to be made to believe them, to take them seriously, to want to act upon them.

The pseudo-historians—trusted because they were, nominally at least, "historians"—would do this important work for the WLP and NRP. The old history was out. It, the pseudo-historians said, had all been written by the rich and the strangers and so was full of lies. The new history was in. It seemed to prove that the rich and the strangers were behind everything bad that had ever happened to the people of The Workers' Paradise and The Racists' Utopia. Essentially, the pseudo-historians remade a handy, soothing, self-justifying folk resentment into the most important historical "truth" imaginable: our suffering is not our fault, but theirs. The leaders of the WLP and NRP knew very well that, having been told the "truth" by trusted "historians," their subjects would wholeheartedly support the elimination of the rich and the strangers, respectively. They were not wrong here. For most folks stood behind the parties as they obliterated the "enemies of the people." Those who didn't simply stood aside and watched in silence.

"That couldn't happen here," Elizabeth assures herself. "I helped build the bulwark against historical bullshit, and I'll be damned if I'm going let any political nut-job tear it down!" This thought eased her concern about the fact that history books go unread, because the fact that they go unread—by masses of people, at least—didn't really make much difference. Sure, she thinks, it would be nice if *From Young Ladies to Wild Womyn* were a bestseller, but that's not important. What matters is that it exists, that it is there on the shelf should it ever be needed. Elizabeth, beneficiary of a liberal education that she is, recalls a bit of Milton: "They also serve who only stand and wait." "That," she thinks, "is what history books like mine do. They stand and wait until such time as they are needed to stop barbarous pseudo-historians from crossing the frontiers of historical truth."

"Nice idea, but a bit too comforting," Elizabeth thinks. She recalls that at least some of those WLP and NRP hackish flacks were not hackish flacks at all, at least in the beginning. They had been trained in the German model, just as she had. Indeed, some were there at its creation. They read the literature thoroughly, posed important questions, travelled to archives to answer them, wrote up the results *sine ira et studio*, and published books some of which can still be profitably read. It's true that they aligned themselves with certain theoretical perspectives, all of which have now been discredited. But they were not rigidly dogmatic like the true hackish flacks. They did not allow their perspectives to do anything but guide their interests and suggest explanations for what they found in the record. If what they found in that record contradicted the theoretical explanations, they generally said so and moved on. They had strong political leanings, but they tried not to permit those leanings to distort the truth they uncovered in the archive.

For all intents and purposes, then, there was little to distinguish these historians from Elizabeth herself. Except, of course, that they worked in the service of evil. How could people trained like her, following all the relevant professional standards, and intent on nothing other than telling it like it really was be so blind to what they were doing? The only answer is that they did not know what they were doing. "That," Elizabeth considered, "is a very scary thought." For if they didn't know they were unknowingly serving evil in writing history the way they did, might it be the case that she too was unknowingly serving evil in writing history the way she did? They were on the "wrong side of history." Was she on the "wrong side of history"? And who gets to decide which "side of history" is "right" and which side is "wrong"?

Who indeed? Today everyone agrees that the WLP and NRP were forces of evil. But Elizabeth, good historian that she is, knows that was not always the case. Several generations ago millions of people—many of them highly educated right-thinking folks just like her—truly believed that the WLP and NRP were forces of good, that they would liberate mankind from war, poverty, oppression, etc. Their ends were fine. Their means, however, were not. For it turned out that destroying the rich and the strangers did not, in fact, really liberate anyone. Quite the contrary. The programs of the WLP and NRP ended precisely in war, poverty, oppression, etc. True, many people foresaw that this would happen. But many did not. And it wasn't as if there was anything obvious that separated those who were on the "right side of history" from those who were on the "wrong side of history" before that history happened. The upper classes rejected the WLP and NRP; the upper classes supported the WLP and NRP. Workers and peasants rejected the WLP and NRP; workers supported the WLP and NRP. The religious rejected the WLP and NRP; the religious supported the WLP and NRP. Most troubling, good historians just like Elizabeth rejected the WLP and NRP; good historians just like Elizabeth supported the WLP and NRP.

Elizabeth recalls a story about the Great Coxswain of The People's Paradise of Inland. A number of years ago a reporter asked him what he thought about the Big Rebellion of 1789. "Too soon to tell," he responded. "That's about right," Elizabeth mutters to herself. From the perspective of the present, it's really quite difficult to tell who will be on the "right side of history" and who on the "wrong side of history." Sure, it's easy to say *now* that the leaders of the WLP and NRP were baddies. They lost. But what if one or the other of them would have taken over the world? What would we be saying about them then? Is there any doubt that we would be saying—with all the earnestness we could muster—that the enemies of the WLP and NRP were the baddies, that the WLP and NRP were always on the "right side of history"?

"Maybe, maybe not," Elizabeth thinks. "What I'm more concerned about now is whether I'm on the 'right side of history.' Will people in 100 years look back on anything I've written with horror and disgust? And if so, what?" Elizabeth considers the question. She figures she's pretty safe with democracy, rule of law, justice, liberty, equality, and peace. These things have been around for a while, most folks seem committed to them, and they are spreading. They are not likely to fall rapidly out of favor the way collectivism and racism did, thereby leaving the well-meaning though clueless WLP and NRP historians standing high and dry on the "wrong side of history."

But she's not so sure about a couple of other issues. Take sexuality, for example. One of her former professors, Albert Kinky, was an early pioneer in the field of the history of sexuality. He wrote a number of path-breaking books on the subject fifty years ago. One such book was *The Deed: A History of Intercourse in Modern Times*. It's a fine piece of research. But in it Kinky almost completely ignores homosexuality of any sort. Where he touches on the subject, he simply says that it's a deviant sexual practice, a kind of illness for which there is no known cure. A few years later Kinky published *The Bond: A History of Marriage in Modern Times*. Again, a fine piece of research. But in it Kinky assumes that the only thing that could conceivably be called "marriage" is a union between a man and a woman. Elizabeth knew Kinky well. He was a good man and a good scholar. Even today, historians of sexuality acknowledge his contributions to the field. But they also say that he was homophobic. And, to a certain extent, he was. But really he was just caught on the "wrong side of history" and didn't know it.

Elizabeth wonders about her friend, Willamina Wellmeaning, who just completed a really good book called *Uncaged Heat: Zoo Reform in Modern Times*. The story she tells is one of liberation. Animals were once locked in small cages where they were miserable and often got sick and died. But then a few enlightened zoologists and officials transformed zoos. They did away with cages wherever possible and attempted to recreate the habits in which the animals naturally lived. The effect was dramatic: the animals appeared to be much happier and healthier. It's an uplifting story. Or is it? Elizabeth knows apparently bright people—the philosopher Petra Prettyvoice, for example—who think zoos in any form are completely barbaric. Whether they hold animals in cages or in pseudo-habitats, zookeepers are essentially enslaving their fellow creatures. If slavery is wrong for humans, it must be wrong for other sentient creatures. Zoos, they say, must be eliminated. Animals must be liberated. We all must be free. To be sure, this is a minority opinion. Nonetheless, Elizabeth can see the logic in it. It's entirely consistent with the *Zeitgeist*. And if the anti-zoo sentiment grows, as she suspects it will, Willamina will be seen as an apologist for something that cannot be apologized for—the cruel oppression of animals. She will be, like Professor Kinky, caught on the "wrong side of history."

Elizabeth is reasonably certain that she is on the "right side of history." Nonetheless the fact that the "right side" sometimes becomes the "wrong side" and the "wrong side" the "right side" bothers her. For how is one to build an effective, permanent bulwark against historical bullshit when what is considered historical bullshit changes all the time? The non-hackish flacks of the WLP and NRP, the kind Professor Kinky, and the wonderful Willamina Wellmeaning all truly thought they were building a bulwark against historical bullshit. Then, however, the "received opinion" on what was historical bullshit and what wasn't suddenly shifted. Not, of course, in the close-to-the-sources empirical sense. What happened is what happened, period. But in the interpretive, storytelling sense. The facts are indeed the facts no matter what a historian thinks about them. The claim "These things happened" is either right or wrong and can be nothing else. The story a historian tells about those things that happened, however, depends on what that historian and those around her think about them. The story has a meaning, a set of implications for life's big questions, that cannot in any strict sense be right or wrong; it can only be meaningful in some particular way to some particular group of people. The facts don't change, but the stories and their meanings do. And therein lies the danger of thinking of history as a permanent bulwark against historical bullshit, for one age's bullshit is another age's bullion.

"Hmm…" Elizabeth thinks, "that's disturbing. Could it really be that there is no *terra firma* upon which to ground our true stories about the past? Is it all 'relative' as the cliché goes?" She considers the question for a moment, for that is all the question requires, and decides that it isn't. The facts are not relative. Anyone who says they are is either a hypocrite, an egomaniac, or insane. Some of the people who say everything is relative fail to register the fact that the proposition "everything is relative" must then be relative too. They are hypocrites. The truth is that some things are a lot more relative than others, and we may yet discover things that are not relative at all. Some of the people who say everything is relative are just shouting, "Look at me! Look at me!" They are egomaniacs. They willfully exaggerate the truth about supposed relativity so others will pay attention to them. Some people who say everything is relative live in an imaginary world they do not know is imaginary. They are insane. They cannot, for whatever reason, see things as they are.

"So what," Elizabeth asks herself, "is the *terra firma* of historical judgment?" She decides that she's not really sure, but that some hot chocolate sounds good.

Chapter 8

Living and Dying with History

Holding a historical resentment is like taking poison and hoping your enemy will die.
—Reinhardt Friedrich Freiherr von Teufel

Elizabeth Ranke, now on her deathbed, is thinking about her life with history books. She's seen them from every angle. She's studied them, researched them, written them, published them and taught them. History books have filled her years. "Now," she thinks, "my years are through." She looks around the room. On her bed stand there are pictures of her mother and father. She loved them. Her diplomas hang on the wall. She's still proud of them. Over on a shelf she sees her dissertation and, next to it, a beautiful jacketed copy of *From Young Ladies to Wild Womyn*. She made a contribution. Greetings and salutations from her colleagues, friends, and former students are scattered before her on the bed. She touched their lives.

"Now," she repeats to herself, "my years are through." She pauses, her mind seeking but not finding any idea on which to land. Then she stops short: "'Now.' That's a funny word 'now.' You say 'now' and by the time you're done it's already 'then.' It's always 'now' and never 'now.' How can that be?" In a flash of intuition, Elizabeth, regular reader of *Scientific Citizen* that she is, thinks about stars. The nearest of them, Proxima Centauri, is over four light years away from our sun; evidence of the most distant star, Gamma Ray Burst 090429B, is around 13 billion light years away. The important point is that in the near case and the far, the news that light carries to us here on Earth is, by the time it gets to us, very old indeed. What we see as "now" is in fact long past. If you were standing on Proxima Centauri, well, you'd be dead because it can't support human life. But if it could, your "now" wouldn't get to us for four years, so that by the time it did, it would be your "then." You couldn't stand on the star that ended as GRB 090429B because it hasn't existed for a long time. But if you could, your "now" wouldn't reach us for 13 billion years, so by the time it did, it would *really* be your "then."

"When we look at the stars, we are looking at the past," Elizabeth concludes. "If that is so," she continues, "when we look at the objects all around us we also must be looking at the past." Again Elizabeth recalls an article she read in *Scientific Citizen*, this one about measuring time. Light travels a bit over 186,000 miles per second; it can go slower, but it can never go faster. Nothing can. Now that seems really fast. But we've already seen that relative to the size of the universe, it's not that speedy. After all, it takes four years for a news-bearing photon to get from Alpha Centauri—our nearest neighbor—to us. You can write a history book in four years, though probably not a very good one. Obviously it takes a lot less time for a photon to get from that pot that will never boil to your eyes. Assuming you are four feet away from said pot, the photon will get from here to there in about four nanoseconds, a nanosecond being 10^{-9} seconds. That's not a long time, but, according to scientists, it's not a short time either. There are, naturally, shorter increments: picoseconds (10^{-12} seconds), femtoseconds (10^{-15} seconds), and Planck units (roughly 10^{-43} seconds). It takes a load of Planck units for news of the watched pot to get to our impatient eyes.

"But," Elizabeth thinks, "it takes even longer for news of that pot to register in our consciousness, if it ever does." According to physiologists (or at least the ones that write in *Scientific Citizen*), fibers like the optic nerve move signals at a rate of about 300 feet/second. That's about the speed of a Formula One racecar, which is pretty fast but not as fast as a photon (roughly 983,000,000 feet/second). Assuming that the pot-bearing signals have to travel three inches from your eyes to the part of your brain that processes vision, it will take .00083 seconds—or 83,000 nanoseconds—for the image to appear in your "mind's eye." The trip from watched pot to consciousness of watched pot is, then, 83,004 nanoseconds, 83,004,000 picoseconds, 83,004,000,000 femtoseconds, and a truly ungodly number of Planck units.

"Everything we sense," Elizabeth thinks, "has already happened. We never experience the present. We only experience the past. What we call 'now' is really always 'then.' We live in history." Elizabeth and her colleagues had often joked that, as professional historians, they lived in the past. Little did she realize that everyone lives in the past all the time. She finds this funny. Many scientists look down on history as being unscientific, and many historians feel bad that history is not more scientific. But there's a sense in which history is the *only* science. For if science is based on experience, and all we can experience is the past, then all sciences must be in some sense historical. Physicists, astronomers, geologists, chemists, biologists, anthropologists, psychologists, sociologists, and political scientists all rely on data that comes from the past. That past may be long ago—billions of years—or that past may be now—billionths of a second—but it is always the past. Elizabeth smiles: "History, queen of the sciences."

Feeling the pain of her coming demise, Elizabeth's smile fades. "Fine," she thinks, "it's always the past, theoretically speaking. But right now it feels to me like *right now*. It's all relative." She's surprised at this thought. It's not a thought she wants to think. She doesn't want to believe that it's all relative to time, the experience of time, or anything else. She still wants *terra firma*, a place where she can stand and see life—past and present—from a vantage point that is absolute.

Many of her colleagues, people she respects, tell her there is no such place. There are laws, but only natural laws, and even these are subject to change. The natural laws that govern physics, celestial mechanics, and chemistry appear to be eternal, but they are only the natural laws of the moment. As circumstances in the universe change, they too will change. The momentary natural laws that govern humankind, they say, are evolutionary laws, the regularities of natural selection. We are the product of evolution, a historical process if ever there were one, and nothing but. Many religious people claim that there is a deity who lives outside time, who created us, who watches over us, and who, because he or she loves us, gave us timeless ethical laws. This comforting idea, her colleagues assure her, is nothing but another evolved response to the harsh realities of life on our planet in our time, like the ability to metabolize proteins, bipedalism, or reason. And evolution itself tells us nothing about the way we ought to live; it simply tells us in a proximate sense why we do live the way we do. The only "ought" in the universe is the "ought" we make for ourselves. We are alone, masters of our own fate.

Elizabeth recalls talking to a group of her colleagues about just this question during a seminar. "If," she asked them, "we as historians are to tell people about the mistakes of the past so they will not have to repeat them, how are we to judge what was a mistake and what wasn't?" One of her number answered that the job of historians was not to judge the past. Historians, the man said, have no expertise in ethics or morals and should not pretend to do so. Rather, historians are trained to examine the artifacts of the past, tell true stories about the past based on those examinations, and tell people those stories so they can decide what was good, bad, or neither. Everyone in the room seemed quite satisfied with this answer.

Except Elizabeth. To her, it seemed like passing the buck. "But how, my friends, are they, the readers of our books, to decide what was good, bad, or neither?" A long silence followed. Finally, another colleague spoke up: "Elizabeth, they will decide based on their laws and the values that stand behind those laws. If they find that something we report in history is consistent with those laws and values, then they will say it is good and be right to do so; if they find that something we report in history is inconsistent with those laws and values, then they will say it is bad and be right to do so. Of course they should follow some rule-bound procedure in deciding these things—what we call 'due process'—but if they do that, then they are on solid ground." Everyone nodded their heads in agreement.

Except Elizabeth. Again, she found this answer unsatisfying. "But," she asked impatiently, "aren't these laws and values historical as well? Don't they exist in time and are, therefore, subject to change? How solid can the ground of historical judgment be if it shifts all the time? There was a moment when many people believed slavery was both legal and consistent with commonly held values. Now most people think they were neither. Nothing about the idea of slavery has changed; only what is considered legal and consistent with commonly held values has. What are people to say to those who practice slavery today? 'No, what you are doing is not wrong in any objective sense, it's just inconsistent with what we think is right at the present moment.' Please, that just won't due." Again, a long silence. Everyone in the room seemed embarrassed that Elizabeth was asking these questions. What place did they have in a historical seminar? After what seemed like a very long time, yet another colleague spoke up: "True, Elizabeth, there are no absolute, ahistorical laws and values. Judgment of this sort, however, is not a matter of momentary laws or subjective values, but of objective consequences. What slaveholders did to slaves was harmful to a great number of people. They did not try to bring the greatest happiness to the greatest number, which is what one should do if one wants to act rightly. We are on firm ground, then, in saying that slavery was bad." Everyone in the seminar seemed to like this answer quite a bit.

Except Elizabeth. To her it seemed to rest on a question that could not be answered. "But how," she asked, "do you measure happiness? The slaveholders seemed to be extraordinarily happy about holding slaves. It's true that the sum total of happiness in Slaveholderland was reduced by the unhappiness of the slaves, but who knows if the sum total of happiness might not have been the maximum possible? If it was, then the slaveholders have to be judged, by your system, very good indeed." Everyone in the room fidgeted uncomfortably as Elizabeth spoke. The chair of the seminar sensed that the situation was getting a bit tense. He politely said, "Well, our time is up. It's been a lively and interesting discussion. Thanks to everyone for coming." And so all departed. Whether they continued to consider Elizabeth's hanging question, she did not know.

But she did continue to consider it. In fact, it consumed her. As she saw it, her professional role was twofold. First, as her advisors taught her and her colleagues agreed, she should endeavor to tell it like it was. The facts were the facts, and her job was to uncover them, tell them in a story, and make sure other people knew that story. On this score, she enjoyed some, albeit limited, success. Her other role, she now thought, was equally important though neither her advisors nor colleagues would seem to agree with her. She needed to tell people not just what happened, but whether it was good or bad. If she did not do this, she could never help guide people to a brighter future. The feminists she wrote about in *From Young Girls to Wild Womyn* were good; she knew that in her heart. The slaveholders of Slaveholderland were evil; she knew that, too, in her heart. But how did she know these things, and on what basis could she explain that knowledge to others?

Her musings were interrupted by the entry of her brother, Martin, into the room. As children, they had never been close; as they aged they grew even more distant. For while Elizabeth followed in her parents' footsteps and became a highly respected professional, Martin strayed. He partied his way through high school, dropped out of a third-tier college to follow a hippie band, "The Happy Deceased," and he ended up living on the streets of Priestly. He was constantly begging money off Elizabeth and, when she refused to give him any more, he started dealing drugs. By that time he had purchased a lot of them, so he knew the business well. Martin's new venture worked out fine until he got addicted and then busted. Two years in jail didn't stop him from using. A child by one of his many girlfriends didn't stop him from using. The contraction of Hepatitis C and a consequent near-death experience didn't stop him from using. He would occasionally call Elizabeth, telling her that he'd cleaned up. But he never had. She tried to help him, but couldn't. She figured she'd just get a call one day from the police saying that they'd found him dead under a bridge.

For most of her life, Elizabeth deeply resented Martin. Like her, he was given everything a child could want: good health, a loving home, fine schooling, opportunities galore. But he threw it all away. He had hurt her and the entire family. She enjoyed telling her friends about her brother the "screw up," the guy who never missed an opportunity to miss an opportunity, who couldn't take "yes" for an answer, who walked halfway only to turn around because he thought the end was too far. She realized that she clung to this story partly because it was true—Martin did have bad judgment—but also because it put her in a good light. The worse Martin was in her telling, the better she looked. Or at least that's the way it worked for a while. In time, though, the story grew old. She had no one to tell it to but herself. And when she told it to herself—and she did so often—she felt no ease at all. What she felt was anger. Martin was bad. He had wounded her. He was the cause of her troubles. Her depression was Martin's fault. Her difficulty in relationships was Martin's fault. Her abiding sense that life was meaningless was Martin's fault. It was all Martin's doing, and it filled her with rage. And when she was rageful, she felt strangely satisfied. She nursed her anger, she enjoyed it, she was fully alive in it.

But how, she thought silently, could she ever be angry at the kind man standing attentively at her bedside? Though he had only a few teeth, his smile was warm. Though his eyes were permanently sunken, he looked at her with evident affection. Though his hands were rough as hide, they stroked her hair lovingly. Though he smelled of cheap cologne and mothballs, he was clean and well dressed. Most importantly, however, he was drug-free and had been since he went to Narcotics Anonymous ten years ago. He'd gotten "the program" after a few false starts and it had changed him. He now worked in a big box store out on the strip, lived in a small apartment, and had a girlfriend he loved. He regularly saw his daughter, now grown, and spent his spare time working with other addicts. He was Martin, but he was not Martin.

Elizabeth gripped her brother's hand. "Hi sweetheart," he said. "You need something?" "No, thanks," she replied. Elizabeth continued to hold on to Martin. She seemed to want to say something but be unable to find the words. Finally, she said, "Martin. I forgive you and I love you." Martin smiled. "Well, thanks, sweetheart. I'm sorry for all the pain I caused you guys, I really am. I did some bad things, Lord don't I know it. I can't fix the past, but I'm trying best I can to walk the right road now. I want you to know that I never intentionally harmed you or anyone. I loved you every minute, even when it seemed like I didn't."

They were silent again. Elizabeth couldn't really explain why she'd said what she said. It made no sense. She recalled her story of Martin, the one she had been telling herself her whole life. It told her that he had treated her cruelly; it told her that he did not deserve to be forgiven and loved; it told her to be angry and to be consumed by that anger. Suddenly, however, it no longer held her in its sway. The facts remained the facts; Martin had done what he had done. Elizabeth knew that. But the very act of forgiving and loving Martin had cast those facts in a different light. Elizabeth recognized that she could still resent what Martin had done. Everyone assured her that there was ample reason to do so. But now that she had forgiven him and expressed love for him, she no longer had to resent him, and in fact she no longer wanted to. She was liberated from this part of the past.

Elizabeth looked out the window. It was autumn, and the leaves were turning from a dull green to bright hues of red, orange and yellow. "They are beautiful even in death," Elizabeth thought to herself. Then, slowly, it occurred to her that Martin had shown her the *terra firma* of historical judgment. It had nothing to do with laws, values or maximizing happiness, as her colleagues thought. It had everything to do with love. Martin had repeatedly hurt many people. That was just a fact, a matter of historical record that no sane person could dispute. But Elizabeth was certain that Martin never intentionally harmed a soul. Quite the contrary, she knew him well enough to be certain that he was a kindhearted person. He always tried to act out of love, albeit with some very mixed results. For many years, Elizabeth refused to see this fact about Martin for it made her uncomfortable. The idea that someone could harm *and* love was too much for her. She found it much more satisfying to invent a self-serving story about Martin, one that explained her own imperfections: "I suffer," so her tale went, "because he does not love me and therefore harms me." But telling that story, Elizabeth now realized, came at a price. She essentially became addicted to it, and progressively more so over time. Once she had controlled the story; it was a convenient excuse for her own troubles. After a time, however, it came to control her; it became a compulsion, a habitual intrusive thought, a kind of spiritual sickness. The only way for her to win her freedom back was to quit the story; the only way to quit the story was to forgive and love Martin. And that, by some mysterious act of grace, is what she had just done. She finally saw things as they truly were: Martin was essentially good, no matter what he had done, because he acted out of love.

This was her historical *terra firma*: one is good, past and present, insofar as one acts out of love for all; one is bad, past and present, insofar as one fails to do so. Examples sprung to her mind. The feminists Elizabeth studied so many years ago were frail, fallible, imperfect people. It could not have been otherwise. They spoke angrily, and they hurt others with their words. They acted violently, and they injured people bodily. They were often blind, and their actions inadvertently resulted in consequences they deeply regretted. Elizabeth had seen with her own eyes that these things were true; they were indisputable facts. But Elizabeth had also seen that virtually everything most Priestly feminists did they did out of universal love. They did not love women only; they loved all humankind—friends and foes, allies and enemies, everyone indiscriminately.

Like Elizabeth's feminists, the slaveholders of Slaveholderland were frail, fallible, imperfect people. It could not have been otherwise. They spoke angrily, acted violently, and were unaware of much. But they did not act out of love for one and all. They divided humankind into those deserving love and those who did not. They loved the former as all people always had, the way a parent loves a child, the way a brother loves a sister, the way a friend loves another. Yet they treated those whom they felt undeserving of love with a special, unique inhumanity. Love is always and always the same; evil is sometimes and always different. Love is a heart; evil is a tumor. In the case of Slaveholderland, the cancer of slavery grew organically within the breast of what had once been a free country. As it gained strength, it took on ever more alien, hideous, and harmful forms. Only quite late did some of the citizens of Slaveholderland realize that it would eventually kill them all unless radical action was taken. At great cost, they made war on the slaveholders. The tumor was removed; the republic was saved; love had triumphed over hate.

In the bright, clear light of this realization, Elizabeth felt no discomfort in believing without any doubt whatsoever that the feminists were good. Yet she wondered about the consequences of saying that the slaveholders were bad. In a certain sense, this conclusion followed necessarily from her newly discovered *terra firma*: if someone failed to act out of love indiscriminately, they were, according to the very rules of logic, bad. But living with history, she thought, is not simply a matter of logic. One must also consider the practical effect of judgments on those who judge. The root of all resentments is labeling someone bad, for that act feeds the natural human tendency to invent comforting stories that explain our suffering. Sometimes, of course, these stories are true. The descendants of slaves do, in fact, suffer today because of the actions of bad slaveholders over a century ago. But, as Elizabeth well knows, all resentment stories—true and false—are addictive. Once the mind latches on to one, it tends to grow, "explaining" more and more of present suffering and crowding out the more nuanced truth of the matter. The resentment-filled stories become, essentially, manias that rule the emotional lives of believers. They are not about what happened anymore; rather, they are about protecting oneself from what is happening now. In this way, people become slaves to history, just as Elizabeth had while she was in the grip of her story about the "bad" Martin. The challenge, Elizabeth thinks, is to make the judgment serve the judge rather than the other way around.

How to do this? For Elizabeth, the answer is clear but a bit disquieting: forgive and love even the bad. On first glance, she thinks, this seems not only impossible but also unethical. Humans are vengeful creatures. They do not easily give up their grudges. Moreover, it seems somehow morally amiss to forgive and love people who enslaved their fellow men not out of love (as if such a thing were possible), but out of greed. Wouldn't doing such a thing encourage others to act in a similar way and therefore make the return of slavery more likely? Elizabeth gives these considerations some thought, and then rejects them both. Surrendering resentments is hard, but it is also possible.

Forgiving and loving "bad" people does indeed have its dangers, but it is worth the risk. And in any case, the only way to free ourselves from the bondage of history and thereby see things as they truly are is to forgive and love. If we do not do this—for the "good" and the "bad"—we will inevitably become mired in resentment stories that will cloud our vision of the present.

It occurs to Elizabeth that it might perhaps be better to simply think of all those who failed to act out of love as ignorant rather than bad. For if Elizabeth has learned anything from writing, reading and thinking about history books, it is that those who have not acted out of universal love simply did not know that love is humankind's only hope for serenity. If everyone hates, no one knows peace. If some hate and some love, some people know peace. If everyone loves, then everyone knows peace. This has been true from the beginning of the human experience, though for much of it humanity did not know it. We walked the Earth as blind men, groping about for relief from our suffering. We found none that was lasting except love for all, past, present and future.

Elizabeth senses a sudden tightness in her chest. She feels pain. But she does not suffer. Her past is unburdened by resentment. Her present is free of anger. Her future is without expectation. She is free as she lets go of life.

Zero Books
CULTURE, SOCIETY & POLITICS

Contemporary culture has eliminated the concept and public figure of the intellectual. A cretinous anti-intellectualism presides, cheer-led by hacks in the pay of multinational corporations who reassure their bored readers that there is no need to rouse themselves from their stupor. Zer0 Books knows that another kind of discourse - intellectual without being academic, popular without being populist - is not only possible: it is already flourishing. Zer0 is convinced that in the unthinking, blandly consensual culture in which we live, critical and engaged theoretical reflection is more important than ever before.

If you have enjoyed this book, why not tell other readers by posting a review on your preferred book site. Recent bestsellers from Zero Books are:

In the Dust of This Planet
Horror of Philosophy vol. 1
Eugene Thacker
In the first of a series of three books on the Horror of
Philosophy, *In the Dust of This Planet* offers the genre of horror
as a way of thinking about the unthinkable.
Paperback: 978-1-84694-676-9 ebook: 978-1-78099-010-1

Capitalist Realism
Is there no alternative?
Mark Fisher
An analysis of the ways in which capitalism has presented itself
as the only realistic political-economic system.
Paperback: 978-1-84694-317-1 ebook: 978-1-78099-734-6

Rebel Rebel
Chris O'Leary
David Bowie: every single song. Everything you want to know,
everything you didn't know.
Paperback: 978-1-78099-244-0 ebook: 978-1-78099-713-1

Cartographies of the Absolute
Alberto Toscano, Jeff Kinkle
An aesthetics of the economy for the twenty-first century.
Paperback: 978-1-78099-275-4 ebook: 978-1-78279-973-3

Malign Velocities
Accelerationism and Capitalism
Benjamin Noys
Longlisted for the Bread and Roses Prize 2015, *Malign Velocities*
argues against the need for speed, tracking acceleration as the
symptom of the ongoing crises of capitalism.
Paperback: 978-1-78279-300-7 ebook: 978-1-78279-299-4

Meat Market
Female flesh under Capitalism
Laurie Penny
A feminist dissection of women's bodies as the fleshy fulcrum of
capitalist cannibalism, whereby women are both consumers and
consumed.
Paperback: 978-1-84694-521-2 ebook: 978-1-84694-782-7

Poor but Sexy
Culture Clashes in Europe East and West
Agata Pyzik
How the East stayed East and the West stayed West.
Paperback: 978-1-78099-394-2 ebook: 978-1-78099-395-9

Romeo and Juliet in Palestine
Teaching Under Occupation
Tom Sperlinger
Life in the West Bank, the nature of pedagogy and the role of a
university under occupation.
Paperback: 978-1-78279-637-4 ebook: 978-1-78279-636-7

Sweetening the Pill
or How We Got Hooked on Hormonal Birth Control
Holly Grigg-Spall
Has contraception liberated or oppressed women? *Sweetening the Pill* breaks the silence on the dark side of hormonal contraception.
Paperback: 978-1-78099-607-3 ebook: 978-1-78099-608-0

Why Are We The Good Guys?
Reclaiming Your Mind from the Delusions of Propaganda
David Cromwell
A provocative challenge to the standard ideology that Western power is a benevolent force in the world.
Paperback: 978-1-78099-365-2 ebook: 978-1-78099-366-9

Readers of ebooks can buy or view any of these bestsellers by clicking on the live link in the title. Most titles are published in paperback and as an ebook. Paperbacks are available in traditional bookshops. Both print and ebook formats are available online.

Find more titles and sign up to our readers' newsletter at
http://www.johnhuntpublishing.com/culture-and-politics
Follow us on Facebook at https://www.facebook.com/ZeroBooks
and Twitter at https://twitter.com/Zer0Books